Melton Mowbray

– From Belvoir to Burrough –

Text by Jenny and Mike Allsop

Paintings by Mike Weston

Cottage Publications

First published by Cottage Publications,
an imprint of Laurel Cottage Ltd.
Donaghadee, N. Ireland 2009.
Copyrights Reserved.
© Illustrations by Mike Weston 2009.
© Text by Jenny and Mike Allsop 2009.
All rights reserved.
No part of this book may be reproduced or stored on any media
without the express written permission of the publishers.
Design & origination in Northern Ireland.
Printed & bound in China.
ISBN 978 1 900935 78 4

The Authors

Born and raised in Harrow, Jenny Gillingham graduated in Geology Honours at Swansea and joined the Geological Survey in South Kensington. Mike Allsop, a native of Essex, also joined the Survey, where he met Jenny and they married in 1973. In 1979, they took the opportunity to escape from the London commuting and moved to the Vale of Belvoir.

Now having time on their hands, they took a three-year course in archaeology and teamed up with other enthusiasts to become the Melton Fieldworkers. They also gave talks to local societies, interviews on TV and radio, community courses on local history and guided tours.

For four years, with their late friend and colleague, Mary Hatton, they published weekly articles on local history in the *Leicester Mercury*. On taking early retirement in the 1990s, they commenced writing up their researches, an activity that is still very much a 'work in progress'.

Jenny Allsop

Mike Allsop

The Artist

Mike Weston spent his early years in Coventry, having been bombed out of two homes during the second World War. At school he enjoyed technical drawing and went on to a career in various aspects of Agricultural Engineering, becoming a Freeman of the City of Coventry along the way.

Having moved to the Vale of Belvoir in 1977, Mike only started drawing and painting again for relaxation. It soon became an all-consuming hobby in his retirement years. Mainly self-taught, Mike gained a lot of his knowledge and skills from Kirby Bellars, Melton and Grantham art groups. His preferred painting medium is watercolour, but he also uses pastels and acrylics.

In 2001 Mike was chosen to be a competitor on Channel 4's *Watercolour Challenge*, painting Anne Hathaway's cottage. More recently, he has helped design a metal sculpture in Melton Mowbray and completed a wall mural for his local hospice where he is a volunteer.

Mike Weston

AUTHORS' ACKNOWLEDGEMENTS

We are most grateful to the following people who kindly allowed us access to their property:

Rebecca Collin (Stapleford Park Country House Hotel), Linda Cox and D. Gibson (King Edward VII School), Major (ret.) P. J. N Downing and Capt. R. I. Chambers, L.G. (Defence Animal Centre), Mr C. Clayton, Churchwarden (St. James Parish Church, Burton Lazars), Messrs Shouler & Son, Auctioneers (Melton Mowbray Cattle Market).

We also gratefully acknowledge the contributions made by past local historians to our understanding of the history of Melton Mowbray, especially Rev. Philip E. Hunt, Mr Jack Brownlow, Mr Trevor Hickman and our friend, the late Mary Hatton, local historian and archaeologist, colleague and co-author.

Contents

The Path to the Present

The borough of Melton occupies approximately the same area of northeast Leicestershire as did the ancient hundred of Framland, the main addition being Asfordby. In the late Anglo-Saxon period, all the freemen domiciled within a hundred would meet monthly as a 'hundred court'. In areas controlled by the Danes, hundreds were known as wapentakes, from the word meaning 'brandishing of weapons', the method by which agreement was signified. Great Framlands Farm, about two miles north of Melton Mowbray, is thought to be the location of the moot-site of the men of the Framland wapentake. Today, the name is perpetuated in the ecclesiastical Deanery of Framland, centred on St. Mary's Church in Melton Mowbray.

In the *Domesday Book,* Melton Mowbray is recorded as Medeltone meaning 'the middle farmstead or village' from the Scandinavian *methal* which possibly replaced the earlier Old English *middel.* This was a most appropriate name since the settlement, located on a river crossing where ancient trackways converge, is at the centre of a large rural hinterland. For about one thousand years, there has been a market here, probably the third oldest in England. Today, farming remains a major part of the economy, and Melton, called the 'Rural Capital of Food', prides itself on its unique and famous pork pies and Stilton cheese. The second element of the name comes from the Mowbray family. They were lords of the manor, first recorded about 1130, who received a royal warrant around 1267.

To the north of the borough is the Vale of Belvoir bounded on the south by a scarp slope, formed from the Jurassic marlstone, and terminated in the north by Belvoir Castle. The Vale villages are located over aquifers from which wells supplied potable water until the last century. Beyond the scarp is a high plateau blanketed by glacial boulder clay and rising to a height of 500 ft above sea level. There are fewer villages here and they depended on water supply from glacial sand lenses. The eastern plateau is underlain by Lincolnshire limestone, part of the Jurassic Ridge, extending from Dorset to the Yorkshire Coast.

The plateau is a vast watershed. To the north streams and rivers drain into the River Trent whilst on the southern side they drain southwards, cutting down into the boulder clay. The River Eye, which rises at Bescaby, becomes the River Wreake at Melton and meanders in its valley down towards Leicester. Settlements here are on terraces of river gravels near lush water meadows. To the south of the River Eye the ground rises to 700ft above sea level at Burrough Hill.

EARLY HISTORY

Understanding of our area has changed dramatically over the last thirty years, in no small part due to the pioneering programme of community archaeology initiated by Peter Liddle. His teams of unpaid enthusiasts can still be found as they search ploughed fields for fragments of pottery or pieces of flint. We now know hominids were perhaps here over 250,000 years ago, and the region was intensely occupied in the Neolithic period. Finds of pottery indicate the presence in the Wreake valley of what could have been the first farming communities.

Excavations at Eye Kettleby located a pair of long mortuary enclosures with a pit containing early Neolithic pottery sherds. Funerary barrows are found along the top of the Marlstone scarp and on the heathland of the eastern plateau. Soil below one excavated barrow near Sproxton suggests forest clearance for agriculture began around 4000 BC. Crossing Saltby Heath are multiple linear ditches, thought to be tribal boundaries. A 2-mile long earthwork, known as King Lud's Entrenchments, has survived and marks the boundary between Saltby and Sproxton. The Welby Bronze Age hoard, discovered around 1875 and rescued from a local foundry as it was about to be melted down for scrap, is one of the most important metalwork finds from the region.

The Iron Age is represented by the great fortified site at Burrough Hill, now preserved within a country park. An ancient trackway, now named the Jubilee Way, connects it to Belvoir. Such trackways hugged the higher ground and were improved during the Roman occupation. Sewstern Lane, dating to the Bronze Age, is the eastern boundary of both Melton Borough and the county. It is now part of the Viking Way to Humberside.

From Tilton, a trackway passed Burrough Hill, crossed the River Eye at Melton and continued to Brock Hill on the scarp overlooking the Vale of Belvoir, joining up with the east-west saltway along the ridge. The road, known by the Saxons as Ferdegate, meaning 'military road', was the main route northwards from the capital and was recorded in the itineraries of medieval kings. Leland, during the reign of Henry VIII, also took this route to London. In the 19th century, locals still called Sandy Lane, south of Melton, the 'London Road'.

The so-called 'saltways' were used to transport salt, obtained from seawater, and used in the preservation of food for the winter. The track along the scarp connected the Fosse Way at Six Hills with Ermine Street in the east and its route appears to have been straightened by the Romans.

When the Roman armies arrived in 43 AD, they found the landscape already occupied by the Corieltauvi. The Romans improved the local agricultural economy, increased production and introduced such innovations as donkey and water mills. Large millstones were recovered from a villa site in the Melton Country Park. Villa estates and farmsteads are plentiful around Melton and at Ab Kettleby Parish Church, the Chancel overlies a mosaic floor and a hypocaust system.

In 1952 at Goadby Marwood, northeast of Melton, a Roman town was recorded during its destruction by ironstone quarrying. Evidence shows that the Romans too had been exploiting the ore. The report tells how the mechanical excavator shattered an urn containing almost 2000 coins. Nearby is the village of Wycomb, a very early name often given to a Saxon settlement next to a small Roman town.

Thus, archaeologists have been able to expand our understanding of this area's history. In St Mary's Way car park, layers of medieval finds around the foundations of contemporary walls overlay flint tools, a Bronze Age funerary urn and pottery sherds from the Iron Age and Roman periods. An early Saxon loom weight was recovered near to the 14th century timber- framed building at the top of King Street. Such finds represent over 4,000 years of continuous occupation in the heart of the town.

<u>The (Not So) Dark Ages</u>

Our region provides rich pickings for the student of place names. The River Devon has a Celtic name, and Wycomb derives from the Latin *vicus* and the Saxon *ham*. Waltham is another early name. The Saxon ending *-tun,* as in Melton, meaning farmstead or village, is common. Following the Danish invasions in the ninth century such places had Scandinavian personal names attached to them, as in Grimston and Croxton. These settlers introduced the suffix *-by,* particularly in the Wreake valley, as in Brooksby. Later the word *-thorp* was used to indicate outlying farmsteads. We also have at Normanton, the village of the Northmen, or Vikings.

Pagan Saxon burials and grave goods discovered in the 19th century brick pits to the north of Melton Mowbray and at Sysonby, suggest a sizeable population. In the Eye Kettleby excavations, archaeologists found 10 post-built Saxon aisled halls.

Early churches constructed of wood have not have survived but in Sproxton churchyard, a 10th century wheel-head cross displays Christian symbols combined with fierce pagan creatures and interlace patterns. Scalford Church is dedicated to the Saxon Saint Egelwin the Martyr, a name unlikely to have a later Norman origin. At Hickling, just over the Nottinghamshire border, a rare Viking hogback tombstone is displayed in the church.

By the eleventh century, Melton had a thriving Saxon market and shared with Leicester the honour of a mint, producing its own coinage. The strategic location, lucrative market tolls and a productive agricultural hinterland made Melton second in importance only to Leicester.

MEDIEVAL TIMES

The *Domesday Book* shows that the manor of Melton included lands in Wyfordby, Burton, Eye Kettleby, Kirby, Sysonby, Eastwell, Welby and Goadby Marwood and had a market paying 20s. The presence of two priests suggests a church already existed and Saxo-Norman pottery sherds have been found in the churchyard. Two watermills, the Beck Mill Holm to the north east of the town and the Corn Mill Holm at the junction of the River Eye and the Scalford Brook, continued working until the late 1800s.

Twelve Domesday villages have since disappeared. Welby Church stands alone amongst earthworks which were once the streets and houses of a thriving community. Similar deserted villages are found at Bescaby, Stapleford and Ringlethorpe, now Goldsmith Grange.

In common with other Norman lords, Roger de Mowbray made grants to religious houses. In Nottingham Street, the Knights Templar were given land for a manor, later occupied by the Knights Hospitaller. The street was known as Spital End until the late 1800s, and remains of boundary walls can be seen in St Mary's Way car park. A 14th century stone arch was reassembled and can be seen in the boundary to Egerton Lodge by the Leicester Road Bridge. The Hospitaller Chapel and graveyard, at the junction of Nottingham Street and Park Road, was used as a tollhouse, surviving into the 19th century. A grant of lands was also made at Burton where the Order of St. Lazarus, a band of crusading knights suffering from leprosy, established its headquarters in England.

The Folville family lived at Ashby Folville Hall. From around 1300 these outlaws, who included a priest among their numbers, terrorised the area for almost 100 years. Their crimes included the murder on the Leicester to Melton road of Roger Beler, Baron of the Exchequer, and the capture of Sir Richard Willoughby, a Justice of the King's Bench, forcing the King to pay the ransom.

In Melton in 1313, timber was stolen from John de Mowbray's new house. A fortified dwelling was no longer required and the new house was set away from the Market. The timber-framed building at the top of King Street has roof beams dating from this period. This hall, open from floor to roof, may be part of the manorial buildings built by John. He was found guilty of treason and in 1322 his lands were confiscated. Five years later, Edward III restored the title and lands to his son and heir, also John, who played host to the King and Queen Philippa when they visited Melton in 1331.

In the countryside, land was put to pasture and Melton became a centre for the lucrative wool market. Wealthy merchants built townhouses and warehouses. The Subsidy Roll of 1327 shows the number of people in Melton paying tax was second only to Leicester, and Walter Prest, one of the country's richest merchants, paid an eighth of the town's total tax. He was granted permission to build a porch on his house so that it jutted out into the Market Place, just as the Swan Porch does today.

In 1339, Melton sent three merchants to a council called by King Edward III at Westminster and the town became one of the centres, or staples, for the control and taxation of wool. Documents record large consignments being exported through several ports including Boston, Bristol and London. The rich guilds of the merchants installed private chapels in the south transept of the Parish Church where piscinas and aumbrys still survive.

AFTER THE DISSOLUTION

Things were to change, however, under Henry VIII, with the destruction of these chantry chapels and the dissolution of the monasteries. The Manor of the Knights Hospitaller, the Priory at Kirby Bellars, Belvoir Priory, Croxton Abbey and the Preceptory at Burton Lazars all went, causing changes to the landscape and social upheaval that was felt throughout England.

One unexpected benefit of this time was the birth of the Melton Mowbray Town Estate. By selling the Church plate, the town's worthies were able buy the lands originally held by the guilds. Further lands were obtained and held by elected feoffees in trust for the town, enabling the long-standing free school to continue. Gradually, the responsibilities of the Town Estate increased until, at the end of nineteenth century, it was able to pass many of them on to the new local government bodies. Today we have the Town Estate to thank for our beautiful parks and other opportunities for leisure.

During the Civil War, Belvoir Castle was besieged and eventually destroyed. Melton became a Parliamentarian stronghold led by Colonel Rossiter. Small skirmishes were common, but one event south of the town left the roundheads severely defeated. It is said that the name 'Ankle Hill' arose from the aftermath when the streets were 'ankle deep in blood', although the name 'Ankelie Hyll' is documented long before the Civil War. It is interesting to note that, during the rule by Cromwell, the parish register for Melton records couples being married at the market cross. Also recorded in the 17th century are several outbreaks of plague, with 343 burials occurring in just one year.

In the countryside, the eighteenth century saw the process of enclosure gather pace which, together with improvements in drainage and animal husbandry, was to lead to a migration to the cities and, from the early 1800s, emigration to the colonies. A legacy of the increasing turn to grassland was the preservation of the ridge and furrow earthworks which are a common sight in the borough and best seen when the sun is low in the sky.

It was the canal mania in the late 1700s that belatedly started the process of industrialization. Loughborough had seen enormous benefits and naturally others wanted a share of the prosperity. Despite the efforts of the Turnpike Trusts, the condition of roads was very poor and those in the Vale of Belvoir could be impassable in winter. The Grantham Canal had some success but the two canals at Melton struggled until the coming of the railways in 1847 lead to their demise. Even so, landowners, including the Duke of Rutland, actively discouraged industrial development and the rural areas suffered.

1800 TO THE PRESENT DAY

By 1801, Melton was no more than a large village of almost 1800 people living within its medieval confines of the River Eye to the south and east and the tollgates to the north and west. The Domesday watermills were still working and life still revolved around the Tuesday markets.

Melton Mowbray was however put firmly on the map by the surge in the popularity of fox hunting. The market place is the meeting place of the territories of the three great hunts, the Quorn, the Belvoir and the Cottesmore. In winter the town became *'one of the brightest and busiest resorts in England.'* At first, around 1787, there was little accommodation and gradually clubs, hotels and lodges were built to house the aristocratic visitors. The railways made access to the town easier and, by the late 1800s the seasonal influx of visitors quadrupled the town's population and 'emergency' stabling under marquees was provided in Play Close. It is difficult for us today to appreciate the social implications of the season at Melton but the town's name became a byword for quality. It also must not be forgotten that it was here that the future Edward VIII first met his wife-to-be, Wallis Simpson.

By the mid-nineteenth century, the increasing population caused severe problems. The river and canal were outflows for the black open sewers in the streets, exacerbated by the livestock markets in the streets radiating from the Market Place.

Wells were often polluted, especially during flooding, and epidemics of typhus and smallpox claimed many lives. Run-down areas such as Gooseberry Square, now Mill Street car park, became notorious breeding grounds for disease.

The sewers were culverted by 1870 when a new cattle market was built outside the medieval boundaries of the town, removing a major source of pollution. Fresh water was piped in from Scalford, but regular and severe flooding, reaching as far as Nottingham and King Streets, still backed up the sewers.

It was not until the 1890s that new industries arrived. Rust's woollen mill and new boot and shoe factories were built. Richard Dalgleish opened an ironstone quarry at Holwell. Later, more were opened on the marlstone plateau and connected by mineral lines to the main rail network. Dalgleish built the Holwell Ironworks near Asfordby with a terrace of workers' cottages. More recently Chappie Ltd arrived in 1951 to become a pet food producer owned by the vast Mars Corporation.

Oil reserves to the north of the town, first exploited during the Second World War, were re-surveyed using new techniques. Producing wells were developed south of Long Clawson and elsewhere in the Vale of Belvoir and still operate today.

A less successful attempt was made to exploit coal in the Vale of Belvoir. Residents, led by the Duke of Rutland, protested against plans to sink shafts in open countryside and so the mine was opened at Asfordby with the main shaft reaching a depth of 250 metres. Geological problems, coupled with a fall in the price of coal, were soon to prove too much to overcome. Sub-surface volcanism had baked and faulted the coal seams. The mine closed after only two years of full production. Thousands watched in March 1998 as 200 kilograms of explosive were used to demolish the mine's towers. It is still debated whether or not the whole project was simply an expensive political exercise doomed to failure from the start.

Today in Melton, narrow building plots in the Market Place, a legacy from our Saxon past, are reflected in the streets, leading south to the magnificent parish church or north along King Street to the timber-framed medieval hall. At the Anne of Cleves, once home to chantry priests, but now a pub, visitors can obtain refreshment, whilst opposite, above the shop-fronts are the bow windows of the houses refurbished for the visiting hunting gentry. And of course there is always the Olde Pork Pie Shoppe.

Walking, cycling and horse-riding through the rural landscape has opened up the ancient tracks and pathways with the villages providing a wealth of history and variety. There are inns, manor houses, medieval churches and timber-framed cottages just waiting to be discovered.

The south side of the market place with its Swan Porch looks much as it did almost two hundred years ago. Then it was immortalised by the artist Henry Alken who recorded a scene from the early hours of 6th April 1837 when a band of drunken aristocrats engaged in a night of riotous behaviour as they proceeded to daub red paint around the town.

Henry de la Poer Beresford, 3rd Marquis of Waterford, was renowned for his outrageous and often malicious pranks. In New York he was imprisoned after a night of rioting to be rescued by the British Consul on payment of $20 to the night watchmen.

On the fateful night during the Croxton Park races, the Marquis led a drunken band armed with pots of red paint. They nailed shut the doors and windows of the Thorpe End tollgate, trapping the keeper inside his reddened house. They then went around the

town, painting houses, shops and the Swan, ripping off brass business plates, breaking flowerpots and windows and they even painted the constables red! One of the rioters was thrown in the Bridewell only for the Marquis to rescue him, threatening to kill the constables. The next evening there was further unrest leading to charges of assault and riot.

As often happened in those times, the watchmen were 'well compensated' and the Court proceedings were held in Derby, away from influence of Leicestershire officials. All were found not guilty of riot but were fined £100 each for assault.

At Easter 1838, the Theatre Royal, Drury Lane put on *The Meltonians,* a play based on Alken's prints. The Marquis married in 1842 and returned to Ireland to live as a country squire eventually to die of a broken neck from a riding accident. Amongst his possessions were found thousands of door knockers and bell pulls!

The Swan Porch was rebuilt after a fire in 1988 and it is claimed that, when the Swan sign was restored, red paint was found under numerous coats of white. Today, to 'paint the town red' means to 'go out and celebrate rowdily', a legacy of the 'Mad Marquis's' night of hooliganism.

The Market Place

MELTON MOWBRAY

M. WESTON. 09

From the Market Place, King Street leads to probably the oldest house in Melton Mowbray. The building, at first sight, appears to be similar to many others in the town but from the rear, a fine timber-framed house is revealed. Based on dendrochronological measurements on a crown post supporting the rafters, the east side has been dated to the 1330s.

This date agrees with a document describing the visit of King Edward III and Queen Philippa to John de Mowbray at his newly built house. It was a time when Melton was undergoing a building boom to accommodate wealthy wool merchants and the new house was built away from the bustle of the market place. The west side is later with a fireplace and internal features from around 1500.

A document of 1540 mentions *le kynges streate* but traditionally, King Street owes its name to a royal visit in 1194. Richard, Coeur de Lion, who spent only a few months of his 10-year reign in England, came to honour William de Mowbray for his loyalty in contributing to the large ransom demanded by Leopold of Austria who had imprisoned Richard as he returned from the Holy Land.

However, William's allegiances changed when King John confronted the Barons. On the Magna Carta of 1215 is the signature and seal, with the crest of a lion rampant (used for the town arms today), of William de Mowbray, Lord of the Manor of Melton and Governor of York Castle. King John had already

stayed in Melton in 1208 and again, for several days, in 1209. In December 1215 he visited the town again, but William, now a rebel baron, was not at home.

Royal visits to Melton Mowbray have continued to the present day and there were many unofficial visits for the hunting season in the 18th, 19th and 20th centuries. A plaque on the Corn Cross commemorates the visit of Queen Elizabeth II in June 1996. The Mayor presented Her Majesty with a pork pie, Stilton cheese and a Hunt cake.

King Street

MELTON MOWBRAY

M. WESTON .09

Anne of Cleves House in Burton Street is one of our oldest buildings. It was probably the dwelling house for the priests of Melton mentioned in the records for 1384. Of this medieval hall, which would have been open from ground to roof with a central fireplace, the stone walls, north window and rear doorway have survived.

In common with St Mary's Church, the house was a possession of the Priory of Lewes in Sussex. During work in the 1990s, archaeologists uncovered possible traces of an earlier building including fragments of green-glazed roof tiles, some in animal form, which would have been on the ridgeline.

The building continued as a chantry house for priests serving the guild altars in the church until 1538 when the Priory was dissolved and its lands, known as 'Lewes Lands', fell into the possession of Thomas Cromwell, the right-hand man of Henry VIII. Tradition has it that Thomas actually lived in the house.

Cromwell's downfall was soon to come. He arranged a marriage for Henry to Anne, daughter of the Duke of Cleve, gaining an ally against France. Henry hated Anne at first sight, calling her a 'great Flander's mare'. He kept his promise to marry her but immediately arranged a divorce. Thomas was tried for treason and beheaded. The Lewes Lands became a part of Anne's generous divorce settlement but there is no record of her visiting Melton.

The building became a Rectory until the mid-1700s when the ecclesiastical ties of 400 years were finally severed. It was leased to local businessmen and the hunting gentry and a sunken cockpit was built to the rear. The Mains of Cocks became legendary; local newspapers reported: *'never it is said so many British noblemen gathered together in a town as at a celebrated Main'.*

In 1934, the Anne of Cleves House was taken over by Elisabeth the Chef and opened as a café restaurant. There you could dine, dance and stay, occupying a comfortable guest room. A succession of owners followed until, in the 1990s, after a grand opening, it found new life as a pub.

Anne of Cleves House

MELTON MOWBRAY

In Saxon times Melton consisted of about 200 people living in mud and thatch cottages huddled around the parish church. The town was always the focal point of a large rural hinterland and the King granted it to Geoffrey de la Guerche, our first Norman lord of the manor. A market was first recorded in 1077 and in the *Domesday Book* it is the only one listed in Leicestershire, being the third oldest in the country. Melton, at an important river and road crossing, had strategic value, but the market tolls, valued at 20 shillings, were also a lucrative asset.

A charter of 1324 set Tuesday as market day and it remains so today. Two annual fairs were also granted. In medieval times, stone crosses were erected where specific commodities were sold. In the centre of the Market Place stood the butter cross, now marked by a replica and a new corn cross marks the site of the original corn market. The beast market was held in Sherrard Street and at the far end was the Sage Cross where herbs and vegetables were sold. There was a Sheep Cross at the top of Nottingham Street and pigs were sold outside the Vicarage at the top of Burton Street. A Women's Market Cross also appears in the records but this could be the same as the Sage Cross.

By the mid-19th century, expansion of the markets was the cause of much concern, especially during the newly introduced fairs when great numbers of animals were brought into the town and polluted ditches lined the streets. By now the Town Estate had bought the manorial rights, which included the right to hold markets. By public demand, it was decided that a purpose built livestock market was required. Local architect, R. W. Johnson was responsible for the design and many of his original buildings still form the core to the market today. The site, on Scalford Road, is leased to the Borough Council for a peppercorn rent and the cattle market continues to thrive, providing both a service to farmers and a great tourist attraction.

The Cattle Market

MELTON MOWBRAY

M.WESTON 09.

The Corn Exchange in Nottingham Street was the product of Victorian efficiency and civic pride. It continued a system for the regulation and taxation of corn that had been part of the market scene since medieval times. Before the Exchange was built, corn was assessed at the Corn Tables on the junction of Nottingham Street and High Street, which was known as Corn Hill. A corn cross, erected in 1996 by the Borough Council, stands near the site of the medieval cross which had disappeared by 1800.

In the spring of 1854, at a public meeting presided over by the Duke of Rutland, it was agreed that a company should be formed. Those who wished to invest in the new corn exchange and function rooms could purchase shares at £5 each. Within a few months, the money was raised and a site in Nottingham Street was bought.

Later that year, the Chairman of Directors of the company William Thorpe Tuxford, led the ceremonial laying of the foundation stone and the following August, the impressive Corn Exchange was officially opened. Built of brick with stone dressings in the Italianate style, it was topped by a polygonal wooden turret. In addition to the large hall for the Corn Market, there were courtrooms, a library, a savings bank and various other offices.

In addition to its function as a Corn Exchange, the building became the venue for many of Melton's social functions. Hunt Balls, dances, orchestral performances and amateur theatrical shows organised by the Earl of Wilton would be held here. In 1926, the Prince of Wales, the Duke of York and Prince Henry attended a dinner of the Melton branch of the National Farmers Union. After both World Wars, celebrations took place in the rooms and the officers and men of the 4th Parachute Brigade were entertained on their return from their epic stand at Arnheim.

In about 1980, the Bell Centre replaced the Corn Exchange and the Bell Hotel. However, the façades of these buildings were retained for the visitor to gain an impression of these imposing old buildings. Above the central arch of the Corn Exchange is a stone roundel showing the Mowbray lion in the centre of a sheaf of corn and around the edge is the name of the company formed in 1854 – The Melton Mowbray Corn Exchange and Public Rooms Company.

The Corn Exchange

MELTON MOWBRAY

YE OLDE PORK PIE SHOPPE

DICKENSON & MORRIS
THE SAUSAGE SHOP

THE HALF MOON

THE HALF MOON

M WESTON · 09.

There has been a church in Melton since Saxon times. Two priests are mentioned in the Domesday survey of 1086 and pottery fragments spanning the time of the Norman Conquest have been found in the churchyard. As the mother church, it has also served chapelries in Burton Lazars, Freeby, Sysonby, Welby and Eye Kettleby. Today St. Mary's is a rare example of a cruciform church with aisles to both transepts, a feature usually associated only with cathedrals.

The earliest fabric, visible in the tower, dates to the time of Roger de Mowbray, around 1150. The patrons, the Mowbrays and the Prior of Lewis, oversaw the completion of the building by about 1330. In the early 16th century Sir John Digby added an upper section to the Tower and a vestry. He also built the incredible clerestory with its 40 windows around both nave and transepts. These add a dimension of light to the church, which is dramatically enhanced on a sunny day.

Dr Thomas Ford arrived in Melton Mowbray in 1773 and stayed as Vicar for almost 50 years. He showed compassion to his flock and, unusually for this time, supported the activities of the non-conformist chapels. Ford's preaching style soon attracted large congregations, the fiery enthusiasm of his words ensuring that no-one was distracted for a moment, even the members of the hunting gentry who attended.

He had a great enthusiasm for music. On journeys to Leicester, he always sang Handel's *Messiah,* starting at the River Eye with the overture. On reaching Brooksby Gate he was into the chorus, 'Lift up your heads', and 'Thanks be to God' at Thurmaston toll gate. He concluded with the 'Amen Chorus' at Belgrave Gate.

On Sunday 5th May 1776, as Dr Ford was preaching, a lightening bolt struck the pinnacles of the tower. A large piece, weighing about five hundredweight, fell through the roof of the north transept. The electricity continued through the bells, down a wire and forced its way through the wall, shattering the fabric. The whole congregation felt an electric shock and ran out into the churchyard. Fortunately, there were no serious injuries.

St Mary's Church

MELTON MOWBRAY

M.WESTON.09

From the 16th to 19th centuries, the endowment of almshouses was a popular form of philanthropy. It was a time when social care was almost non-existent and cessation of work often led to destitution. Various Poor Relief measures attempted to raise money from the households in each parish, but it was often left to generous benefactors to help.

One such benefactor was Robert Hudson who was born in Melton in 1564. Hudson went to London as a young man and became a leading merchant in the City Guild of Haberdashers. He maintained his ties with his home town and was to become Lord of the Manor of Melton. His will dated 1638 provided for the building and endowment of the almshouses, or Bedehouses, in Burton Street.

Robert Hudson's bequest gave housing to six poor bachelors or widowers. It also specified that the occupants be paid the sum of £3.5s quarterly and £3 at mid-summer to buy winter coal. Ten shillings was paid for one of the men to read prayers twice a week and money was set aside for a yearly meal. One shilling in bread was also to be distributed to the poor each Sabbath-day.

Later benefactions enabled the provision to be extended to accommodate six poor ladies. In the 1840s a large central space on the upper floor, originally the dining area, became the town's museum and library. Opposite the Bedehouses, a set of stone steps in the roadside wall allows easy access to the Parish Church. To the rear, a large well-tended garden is a haven of peace overlooked only by the tower of St. Mary's Parish Church.

Today, a Trust continues to manage the modernised, self-contained flats. Over the front door of the mellow ironstone building is an inscription which reads *Maison Dieu, 1640* and, written on a large beam in the lower corridor, *R.H. 1640* reminds the occupants of their original benefactor.

The Bedehouses

BURTON STREET

M.WESTON.09

The parkland in the heart of the town is provided by the Melton Mowbray Town Estate. From its foundation over 400 years ago, this ancient institution has acted through its elected feoffees and townwardens on behalf of and for the benefit of the townspeople. Now a registered charity, it has as its emblem the Mowbray arms: a white lion rampant (facing left) on a red background, differenced with a cross and fleurs-de-lys, to represent the guilds from which it originated.

Christopher Draper was a Melton man, a successful ironmonger who became an Alderman of the City of London. In 1553, he owned the lordship of the manor of Melton and in 1560 was elected Sheriff of London. Queen Elizabeth I conferred a knighthood on him when he became Lord Mayor in 1566. Melton celebrated, buying *'lam, motton and chikings'* for Alderman Draper. Sir Christopher had three daughters, Benedicta, Brigitt and Agnes and each of them was to marry a future Lord Mayor.

After the dissolution, Draper had somehow acquired the Guild lands around Melton; and these were purchased to become the nucleus of the Town Estate. The Crown challenged this ownership unsuccessfully, firstly in 1566 and again in 1577, when it was claimed that these were 'concealed lands', that is, lands that should have reverted to the King.

Rents from these and other lands originally funded a schoolmaster for the free Grammar School. Later, other responsibilities were taken on including repairs to bridges and roads, the water supply and street lighting and a school for girls. In 1849, the Town Estate bought the lordship of Melton, which included the right to the market tolls.

Local authorities now run many of these services but the Town Estate is still responsible for the street markets. It also provides parks and recreational facilities including two sports grounds and a golf course. The parkland has expanded over the years to include Egerton Park and the Town War Memorial. It offers a peaceful haven from the hustle and bustle of the Market Place, one that undoubtedly would not have survived without the efforts of this unique institution.

The Town Estate

MELTON MOWBRAY

M.WESTON.09

The Melton Mowbray Pork Pie was made famous by the winter visitors, so much so that, as early as 1831, supplies were sent by stagecoach down to London. Jealous of their 200-year-old reputation, the Melton Mowbray Pork Pie Association has recently gained Protected Geographical Indicator status from the European Commission. Pies bearing the town's name must be made in its vicinity using traditional ingredients, namely seasoned, coarsely chopped, uncured pork, which is grey in colour after cooking, moistened with bone jelly. The hot water crust pastry walls are unsupported in the oven and so sag to give the pie its unique appearance.

In the winter of 1877, Melton was overflowing with royalty and nobility from all over Europe. A *Daily Telegraph* reporter, describing a factory tour, wrote:

> '*is not Melton Mowbray celebrated from the Indies*
> *to the Pole for its raised pies, and do not the firms of*
> *Collins and Co … dispatch thousands of these delica-*
> *cies to all parts by the morning passenger train?'.*

Collins & Co commenced making pork pies at Burton End around 1860 and in 1880 they built an imposing brick factory in the Victorian style. In its centre is a tall round headed carriage arch and there were new offices and more ovens behind the new façade. The firm survived until 1919 when it was bought and closed down by Evans & Co. Later, Sutton Brothers, pork butchers and pie makers, traded there for 50 years from 1922.

Melton Mowbray now calls itself the 'Rural Capital of Food' and the flagship producer is Dickinson and Morris, based at the Olde Pork Pie Shoppe in Nottingham Street, which John Dickinson first rented in 1851. Since a bad fire in 1991, it has been owned by Samworth Brothers who, through superb marketing and, of course, an excellent product, have greatly increased the demand for our traditional pies. At the shop, visitors can see hand-raised pies being made and, not only can they buy pork pies, Stilton cheese and sausages but also on sale is the traditional Hunt Cake, a rich fruit cake made to the original 1854 recipe.

Collins & Co of

Burton Street

MELTON MOWBRAY

The first mention of a school in Melton Mowbray occurs in 1347 when Edward III confiscated the possessions of the Priory of Lewes. Education then seems to have been undertaken by the religious guilds until these were dissolved. In 1549, the Town Estate endowed a school within the town of Melton and continued to be responsible until the state took over in 1891.

The King Street schools, run by the Town Estate, were opened in 1818 with a procession from the Church. The Melton Harmonica Band led the Vicar and Churchwardens who were followed by 180 boys and 210 girls. John Brereton, the schoolmaster, wrote in his diary: *'29th January, opened new school in King Street…had previously taught in the church 5 months 24 days'.*

Brereton, appointed in 1810, was Melton's first schoolmaster without a theology degree. He taught the three Rs, geography, science and natural history and would entertain the public with his innovative magic lantern shows. He was particularly fascinated by electricity and, after a visit to the Dowager Duchess of Rutland, wrote in his diary, *'the Duchess is electrified'.*

Brereton also describes a lightening strike on Watchorn, a shepherd, on 24th May 1824,

'He was hurled into eternity by an element which although so destructive in its passage to earth may in this vast system of the universe be the means of purifying the air'.

In the *Grantham Journal,* he writes that Watchorn was *'blackened by the voltaic action, his fork twisted in the heat and the hobnails driven through the soles of his boots'.* He collected £5 for Watchorn's widow by exhibiting the burnt clothes on market day.

A respected and valued schoolmaster of the 'new scientific age', John Brereton retired in 1845 after 34 years of teaching.

Set on Burton Hill with its clock tower dominating the view, the County Grammar School of King Edward VII was opened on 13th January 1910 with great ceremony. It had been so named with the specific permission of King George V. After many speeches and the singing of the National Anthem, the assembly then sat down to tea provided by Alderman Richard Dalgleish and his wife.

King Edward VII School

MELTON MOWBRAY

M.WESTON.09

This peaceful scene near the junction of the River Eye and the Scalford Brook is in the centre of Melton near the pet food factory and close to the railway line. Much of Melton's industry has been located on the east side of town, down wind from the residential districts.

In 1793 an unsuccessful attempt was made to open a frame-work-knitting shop in Park Lane. The preserved building, near to the churchyard, is easily recognised by its two storeys of almost continuous 9-light windows around an enclosed yard.

By the end of the 19th century unemployment was of great concern and, in 1896, a new woollen mill was built very near to the site of a Domesday watermill, continuing Melton's long association with the wool trade. Three storeys high, it was located off Mill Street by the river as water was essential for the steam engines. Its tall chimney could be seen for miles. Owned by Messrs T. J. Rust & Co of the Wyvern Group of Spinning Mills, it was soon to employ hundreds of local girls.

In 1951, part of the site was sold to Chappie Ltd. The new factory expanded and today, Pedigree Masterfoods (Division of Mars UK) is one of the largest employers in the area. Flanking the footpath alongside the Scalford Brook towards the River Eye is a high wall, once part of Rust's mill and now incorporated into the factory complex. Nearby Wyvern Terrace is another reminder of the steam mill as are the remnants of sluice gates that controlled the flow of water. On the banks of the River Eye, there are a few mounds and a leat from the old watermill that had worked for over 800 years.

Although the mills have long gone, the town's association with good quality woollen cloth has remained. The term Melton Cloth is still used today for a heavy worsted cloth, closely woven with a smooth surface to provide a compact and weatherproof material. For the inauguration of the American President, the then First Lady, Hillary Clinton, wore a coral coloured coat of Melton Cloth to combat the inclement weather.

The Wool Mills

MELTON MOWBRAY

M.WESTON.09

The imposing red brick façade of the house next to the George Hotel in High Street hides an older building dating back to the reign of William and Mary. The fourth storey, now demolished, and limestone cornices, architraves and quoins made this one of smartest and tallest in Melton. Inside, the 17th century staircase, fireplaces and wood panelling made it a home from home for visitors in the winter hunting season when accommodation was at a premium. The house, because of its popularity with the Scottish gentry, was known as the 'Thistle' and was to become home to a sharpshooter and horseman of great renown.

In 1799 Hercules Ross returned from Jamaica and built Rossie Castle near Montrose in Scotland. His son was born in 1801 and Hercules wrote to his life-long friend Vice-Admiral Horatio Nelson, congratulating him on a famous victory at the Battle of Copenhagen and begging him to visit Rossie Castle and to be godfather to his son. Nelson accepted the invitation, writing: *'You do not think me capable of forgetting when your house, carriages and purse were open to me, and to your kindness I probably owe my life'.* So it was that Ross Junior was christened Horatio in the Admiral's honour and raised as befitting the laird's eldest son.

In the 1820s, the now Captain Horatio Ross of the 14th Light Dragoons came to the Thistle. As the leading pistol shot and member of the famous Red House Club in Battersea, this brawny highlander was the man to beat. In Melton, he won the local pigeon shoots organised by Mr Webster, Melton's gunsmith. He often passed the time shooting at the town cats and the pigeons on the rooftops.

Opposite the 'Thistle' was the 'Shamrock' where the Irish gentry stayed. On it a fire insurance plaque showed a small figure of 'Hope'. As a newspaper reporter approached the Thistle, Ross leaned out of the window and shouted, "you shall see me take the head off". Having hit the left breast of 'Hope', he declared, "that will not do!" and shot the head clean off!

A Sharpshooter in the High Street

MELTON MOWBRAY

M. WESTON. 09.

Thomas Egerton, 2nd Earl of Wilton, had a family seat at Heaton Hall near Manchester. He married Lady Mary Stanley, daughter of the 12th Earl of Derby and the couple became known for their lavish parties. The Earl, who was an expert horseman with a passion for hunting and horse racing, founded the Heaton Park races in 1827. In 1828 they bought Park House and 15 acres of land in Melton, next to the River Eye. The fashionable architect, James Wyatt, who was working at Belvoir Castle, was commissioned to build a new hunting lodge with formal gardens alongside Park House.

The Wiltons became 'King and Queen of Melton' and continued to entertain lavishly. Amongst the guests were the Prince of Wales, the Duke of Wellington and Disraeli. The diaries of Princess Mary, great-grandmother to our present Queen, describe frequent visits to Egerton Lodge. The Earl, patron of the Melton Theatre and closely involved with the Melton Dramatic Club, wrote plays and gave musical performances, with which he entertained both at private parties and at public performances in the Corn Exchange in aid of charity.

The Earl's wife died in 1859 and he married Isabella Smith, staying in Melton until his death in 1882. Lady Wilton remained at Egerton Lodge until her death in 1919, latterly with her new husband, Arthur Pryor of Hylands, Essex. In 1928, the Wilton Estate was auctioned in three lots, the brochure describing the Lodge as,

'exceptionally well placed in the finest position in the centre of the 'fox hunting metropolis'… a few minutes' walk of the London Midland and Scottish and London and North Eastern railway stations whence London can be reached in two hours'.

Park House was demolished to build Wilton Road and, for 40 years, the Lodge became the Council offices and the Back Park is now a car park and a library. The formal gardens, part of which serves as a War Memorial, the parkland with mature trees and the playing field beyond the River Eye became the property of the Town Estate for the benefit of the townspeople of Melton.

Egerton Lodge

MELTON MOWBRAY

M·WESTON·09.

At the south end of Burton Street, near the railway bridge, is a grand Georgian house with a large portico. Cardigan House, originally Ivy House, was the winter hunting quarters of James Brudenell, 7th Earl of Cardigan. The Earl achieved immortality by leading the disastrous Charge of the Light Brigade at Balaclava in 1854 and for the woollen jacket he wore, now known as a cardigan.

He and the young Adeline Louise de Horsey scandalized society by setting up home whilst his wife lay dying at the family seat of Deene Park, Northamptonshire. Brudenell and Adeline were eventually married in 1858 but their very public pre-marital affair made them unacceptable in polite society and greatly disapproved of by Queen Victoria.

Adeline was a great beauty and a very competent painter who loved music and dance. Passers-by would stop and listen to her singing though the open windows. After 10 years of marriage, the Earl suffered a fatal riding accident leaving Adeline to play the part of the merry widow. She set her cap at Benjamin Disraeli, who was greatly relieved when Adeline married Don Manuelo, Count de Lancastre, in 1873.

After just 6 years they parted company and in 1883, Adeline bought Ivy House outright. As time passed, the Countess grew ever more eccentric. A contemporary account in the ladies magazine *Queen* described her sitting on the balcony overlooking Burton Street. Her face appeared *'coated with a thick coat of pink enamel'*; a thin muslin strip was tied tightly around her nose and around her brilliant eyes were painted large black circles. Poised on her wig of chestnut curls was a jockey cap of peacock feathers. The small dog on her lap was dressed to match the day's outfit.

Adeline commissioned a carpenter at Oundle to make her a coffin. She would take this macabre item wherever she travelled. In Melton, it was set upright in the hall apparently to shock any visitors. At times, Adeline would put on a bright blue dress and stand inside it. Adeline eventually died in 1915 at the great age of 92 years.

Cardigan House

MELTON MOWBRAY

M.WESTON.09.

The problem of the poor was one that greatly troubled society. Melton's vestry minutes describe how strangers were deterred from returning to the town, *'payde to a pooreman and his wyff that was whypte and went to Buckminster'*. The Poor Law Amendment Act (1834) allowed parishes to form Unions to offer help through Workhouses. These were to be *'uninviting places of wholesome restraint'*.

The Melton Union Workhouse on Thorpe Road was built for 300 paupers from Melton and 54 parishes. It was designed by Charles Dyer, a London architect, whose best work was in Bristol, where his Victoria Rooms are an important feature of the city. The Workhouse was on a rare elongated-H plan in the late classical style and a circular plaque in the gable reads *'Charles Dyer, 1836'* with, around the edge, *'Melton Union Workhouse'*.

The sexes were strictly segregated and all children and able-bodied adults were made to work. Relief was only for those unable to do so. In 1870, R. W. Johnson designed and built an

infirmary block behind the main building. About the same time, a block for vagrants was erected outside the walls of the workhouse. Considered a bad influence on inmates, vagrants were kept completely separate. They had to work in return for a night's shelter.

A few years ago we entered the cold, dark corridor of the vagrants' block where a small washroom at the far end offered a chink of daylight. Cell doors were still fitted with locks, spy holes and a trapdoor; each cell window still held a chained bolt. Breaking rocks for roadstone was men's work; the fragments being passed through grids, now blocked, to the outside.

The regime ended with 20th century reforms and, like many others, the hated workhouse was made into a hospital. With the building of a new Melton Hospital at the rear of the Infirmary block, the buildings designed by Charles Dyer and R. W. Johnson have an uncertain future. The cells are deteriorating rapidly and Melton may soon lose this rare survival that reminds us how harsh and unforgiving social attitudes were in the not so distant past.

St. Mary's Hospital

MELTON MOWBRAY

M·WESTON.09

The Market Place of Melton Mowbray is the neutral meeting point of three great Hunts, the Belvoir, the Cottesmore and the Quorn. It is of no surprise that the town became known as the 'Metropolis of Hunting', attracting the nobility and royalty of Europe for the season.

A notable visit came in December 1843 when Queen Victoria and Prince Albert stayed at Belvoir Castle. Other distinguished guests included the Dowager Queen Adelaide, the Duke of Wellington and many members of the nobility.

The meet of the Belvoir understandably attracted great interest and there were several thousand persons present at Croxton Park, the redcoats of the huntsmen mingling with the immense moving mass. Prince Albert was accompanied by the Duke of Wellington and guided by Lord Wilton as the mounted throng accompanied the royal carriage to the Spinneys on the outskirts of town. Here the Master, Lord Forester, brought the hounds to Her Majesty for inspection.

Prince Albert rode well with the Hunt and every detail was reported in the national press. Later, Victoria wrote to her uncle, King Leopold: '*One can scarcely credit the absurdity… Albert's riding so boldly has made such a sensation… they make much more of it than if he had done some great act*'. The Queen was definitely not amused!

The next day the Royal couple, escorted by mounted members of the Hunt and the local gentry, left Belvoir and drove to Melton. Here they were greeted by peals from the church bells and streets lined with people. The procession entered under a triumphal arch of sporting emblems, surmounted by the Union Jack and the words '*Welcome Victoria*'. Approaching the Market Place another arch proudly bore the St. George's ensign with '*Albert, Prince of Wales, England's Hope*' and, further on, yet another proclaimed '*Peace and Prosperity*'. At the western end of town, outside Lord Wilton's home, a magnificent arch displayed the Royal Arms with '*God Save the Queen*' above. Nearby, 800 schoolchildren cheered the Royal couple and were later rewarded with a bun each in the yard of Egerton Lodge.

The Hunts of Melton

THE VALE OF BELVOIR

M.WESTON 09

Cheese has been a part of man's staple diet since animals were first domesticated. In Melton Country Park fragments of pottery sieves used in cheese-making were found which archaeologists dated to the Roman period. It was in the 18th century when Melton's blue-veined cream cheese first became famous, albeit by the name of Stilton, a small town on the Great North Road (A1).

There are several claimants for the title of originator of Stilton cheese but it is generally agreed that Mrs Pawlett of Wymondham was the first to standardise production and that she sent supplies to the Bell Inn at Stilton. From there its fame spread and Stilton became the king of English cheeses. Its name was first mentioned in 1722 and it survived the nineteenth century suggestion to rename it 'Meltonian cream cheese'.

The Stilton Cheese Makers Association was founded in 1936 to maintain quality and to protect the name of Stilton. Now, by law, Stilton can only be made at authorised dairies in the counties of Leicestershire, Derbyshire and Nottinghamshire. In Melton Mowbray, the only factory remaining is Tuxford and Tebbutt. Most of the village dairies have closed, but the co-operative at Long Clawson, set up in 1911 by 12 village farmers, is still a successful business. At Quenby Hall, where a blue-veined product known as Lady Beaumont's cheese was made, the manufacture of Stilton has been revived in the newly refurbished dairy. Sadly, the dairy at Hartington in Derbyshire is in the process of closing, bringing the number of present day producers down to only six.

In the late 19th century, Henry Morris controlled several dairies including the large, purpose built factory on North Street in the centre of Melton. His village concerns included Saxelbye, now the oldest surviving Stilton producer. After his death in 1919, the prize-winning dairy was sold to the Webster family and it is still known as Websters today. The roadside scene has changed little over the years. Workers, in their white protective clothes and headgear, still sit on the wooden veranda next to the seventeenth century cottages that house the offices.

Webster's Dairy

SAXELBYE

M. WESTON ·09

Belvoir Castle stands on the eastern end of a spur with spectacular views over the Vale of Belvoir. This is the fourth castle to be built on the site since Robert de Todeni, a Breton and standard-bearer to William the Conqueror at the Battle of Hastings, first saw this 'bel veder' or 'beautiful view' and built his stronghold. Eventually, the Lordship came to Isabel and, with her marriage to Robert de Ros of Hamlake in 1247, Belvoir became the possession of the de Ros family. This continued until Eleanor de Ros, who married Sir Robert Manners of Etal, became heir to the estates in 1509. Their grandson, Sir Thomas, was created 1st Earl of Rutland in 1526 and in 1703, John Manners, the 9th Earl was created 1st Duke of Rutland.

Todeni's Norman castle was built here primarily for defence although this was rarely tested in medieval times. However, it was severely damaged during the Wars of the Roses, worsened by the activity of Lord Hastings who took stone to build his own castle. Thus, the 1st Earl was faced with a derelict building that he commenced to rebuild in 1528. During the Civil War, Belvoir was a Royalist stronghold on which Cromwell took revenge and the castle was razed to the ground by his troops in 1649.

The replacement, designed by John Webb and completed in 1668, was an undistinguished four-square mansion. It was not to the liking of Elizabeth, the fifth Duchess who, in 1801, engaged the services of James Wyatt to create the mock medieval castle we see today. Notwithstanding the death of Wyatt in 1813 and a major fire in 1816, the castle was finally completed in 1830.

The tranquil surroundings of Belvoir Castle in the heart of rural England are now a major tourist attraction and have been the setting for many Hollywood films and period dramas. The Castle remains the home of the Manners family where, in 2009, David, the 11th Duke of Rutland, together with the Duchess and their children, are celebrating the 500th anniversary of the Manners family at Belvoir.

Belvoir Castle

VALE OF BELVOIR

M. WESTON. 09.

After the Boer Wars when an estimated 350,000 horses were killed, steps were taken to improve the supply of horses to the Army. These included the establishment of a depot on the west side of Melton. A failing stud farm, built in 1895 in the middle of open fields, was an ideal solution and the Army Remount Service first occupied this stable block in 1903. Cavalry officers in Melton for the hunting season often remarked that waking up to the noise of hooves clattering along the cobbled streets reminded them of army camp.

The Royal Army Veterinary Corps (RAVC) was founded in 1796 and during the Second World War it became responsible for dogs, as well as horses. In 1942 the RAVC and the Remount Service were amalgamated and, by the end of the War, was responsible for all management of animal resources. It was found that the Melton establishment was ideal in terms of both location and facilities and in 1946 it became the base for the Corps, which included Schools of Equitation and Farriery and a Veterinary Hospital. The Dog Training School is now an integral part of the work where specialist sniffer dogs and their handlers are trained to detect drugs, guns, buried mines and human remains. In 1991, there was further reorganisation when the Defence Animal Centre was formed.

Public awareness of the Centre was raised when a badly wounded horse captured the heart of the nation. On 20 July 1982, as the Queen's Lifeguard left Knightsbridge Barracks, an IRA nail bomb exploded, killing 2 soldiers and 7 horses. Sefton, a large Irish-bred ceremonial drum horse, underwent 8 hours of surgery for a severed jugular vein and about 30 shrapnel wounds. During rehabilitation at Melton, regular bulletins on his progress were published. Sefton recovered and went back to duty before his well-earned retirement. His marble headstone now stands at the Defence Animal Centre.

The Royal Army Veterinary Corps was granted the Freedom of the Borough of Melton on 29th September 1977. During the ceremony bands played suitable quick marches – *Drink Puppy Drink* and *A-hunting we will go!*

The Defence Animal Centre

MELTON MOWBRAY

M.WESTON 09

Stapleford Park was the seat of the Sherard family, who became the Earls of Harborough, for almost 500 years. In 1894, it was purchased by the Gretton family who built, amongst other things, the south front and the new stables. Following the death of the second Lord Gretton in 1982, the house was sold to Bob Payton who converted it into a luxury hotel. Mr Payton was responsible for introducing the deep pan pizza to England.

The Old Wing of the Hall was built about 1500 and restored by Lady Abigail Sherard who was *'an admirer and collector of antiquities'*. She embellished it with Dutch gables and decorated the whole with canopied statues. An inscription proclaims *'William Lord Sherard repayred this building AD 1633'*. A much smaller plaque states *'And Bob Payton did his bit, AD 1988'*.

The most famous Sherard was, perhaps, the 6th and last Earl of Harborough. In 1844, when the Midland Railway wished to construct a line over part of Stapleford Park, he refused permission for the surveyors to enter his land. Signs were posted around the estate warning railway surveyors not to trespass. Even the offer of a private station could not change the Earl's resolve.

What then ensued became known as the Battle of Saxby.

On 13th November 1844, a party of surveyors was taken prisoner. The next day the railwaymen, reinforced by navvies and three prize fighters from Nottingham, were confronted by a barricade manned by forty or so of the Earl's men. The surveyors were again repelled and the skirmishes became more violent with men injured.

A year later the first fatality occurred when His Lordship ran over and killed a goat. In June 1846, an Act of Parliament authorised a new route curving sharply around the estate. This became known as Lord Harborough's Curve.

In 1953, Lord Gretton opened the house and gardens to the public. A miniature railway, two model liners on the lake and a lion reserve became further attractions. In 1982, the railway was put into storage until a group of enthusiasts, led by Lady Gretton, restored the line and re-opened it in 1995.

Stapleford Hall

NR MELTON MOWBRAY

M. WESTON. 09.

When driving through back roads of the Vale of Belvoir you can suddenly come across small hump-back bridges. Occasionally, a lock and keeper's cottage can be found and, near villages, the remains of wharves have survived. The Nottingham to Grantham Canal, built in 1797 to connect the Trent Navigation to Grantham and the Wash, was finally closed in 1936. Cheap coal, nightsoil for the fields and other commodities were brought in and local produce could now reach a wider market. Today, an active band of enthusiasts is restoring and maintaining the waterway for leisure purposes.

In Melton, by contrast, few signs of the busy basin lined with wharves at the bottom of Burton Street can be found. An avenue of trees and a pair of lock gates in the nearby park mark the route of the infilled canal. The Boat Inn stands as a rare reminder of this time and the landscape to the east and west of town still bears traces of the Wreake Navigation and the Melton to Oakham canal.

At a town meeting in the White Swan Inn, plans for the Wreake Navigation linking Melton and Leicester were first discussed. Viscount Melbourne (Lord of the Manor), the Duke of Rutland and the Earl of Harborough were amongst the proprietors; the architect was Christopher Stavely. Opened in 1797, the canal was built with unusually wide locks to accommodate broad beam barges and the basin, surrounded by wharves, was connected to Oakham in 1803 providing an economic lifeline for the whole region.

The brief hey-day of the canals ended abruptly in 1847 with the construction of the Midland Railway. The Oakham Canal suffered in summer from problems of water supply and the owners sold out to the railway. Extraordinarily, the owners of the Navigation failed to appreciate that much of their revenue came from through traffic to Oakham. They decided to soldier on but eventually had to admit defeat and the Navigation was closed in August 1877. Within 5 years, the basin was filled in but the warehouses continued in use for the storage of the luxuries demanded by the hunting visitors.

The Canals of Melton Mowbray

MELTON MOWBRAY AND THE VALE OF BELVOIR

Burton Lazars, just a mile outside Melton Mowbray, owes its name to the medieval crusading Order of St Lazarus. Here, a large earthwork site is all that remains of their headquarters in England. Although the Knights were responsible for those suffering from leprosy, there is no evidence that lepers actually lived here.

Across the road in the peaceful churchyard of St James is a vault belonging to the Zborowski family who, due to Hollywood, will never be forgotten.

Count William Elliott Morris Zborowski, an American millionaire of Polish descent, had a fascination with speed. He was a keen huntsman and in 1886 he purchased Coventry House in Burton Street, ideal with its stabling for 21 hunters. He became well known for his splendid hospitality and took part in the famous Midnight Steeplechase. He married in 1892 but the Count and Countess Margaret were heartbroken when their 3-week-old son, Martin Ladislas, died in 1893. He was buried at St James Church, Burton Lazars. In February 1895 a second son, Louis Vorow was born.

In 1899, the Count's love of speed led to an obsession with a new invention, the motorcar. Racing was a dangerous pastime; cars were liable to explode or turn over without warning and fatal accidents often involved the spectators. Aged just 45 years, he was taking part in the hill-climb from Nice to La Turbie on April 1, 1903. The car hit a wall, killing him instantly.

The Count's body was returned to Coventry House and he was taken for burial to Burton Lazars. Melton came to a standstill, shops closed and the road to Burton was lined with mourners.

The Countess died in 1911 leaving the young Count Louis with both his father's wealth and his obsession with speed and motorcars. He contributed to the foundation of Brooklands and was a director of Aston Martin. He designed and built his own cars, amongst them the enormous aero-engined racers known as Chitty Bang Bang.

Count Louis also died in a motor racing accident, in the Italian Grand Prix at Monza in 1924, aged 29 years. St James was filled with flowers; one magnificent wreath was addressed to 'my dear friend' and came from Queen Alexandra. Today, two gilded bronze 'wreaths' hang inside the Parish Church.

Chitty Bang Bang

BURTON LAZARS

M·WESTON·09.

In 1811 a racecourse was built at Croxton Park, the Duke of Rutland's hunting box. Prior to this, many a match had been made over the dinner table when the relative merits of mounts were discussed. One occurred in 1790 when Mr Hardy challenged Mr Willoughby for 1000 guineas. The nine-mile course was from Melton to Dalby Wood. Such cross-country matches became known as steeplechases.

The fox hunting purists were antagonistic towards steeplechasing but around 1840, the Melton Hunt set up a course at Burton Lazars. This was ideal with field fences and a water jump over the Burton Brook. Nevertheless, by the 1860s, the sport was dying out. In 1863, the National Hunt Committee drew up new rules and co-opted Lord Grey de Wilton to their number. They were soon to handle a dispute when the Grand National Hunt Steeplechase was run the following year in Melton.

For many years the Croxton Park and Burton races were run together. On race day, the town was filled to overflowing. Goods traffic was halted and railway lines closed as a continuous stream of carriages, often in fine livery, descended on Burton. At dawn carts, laden with food and drink, rattled along the dusty track towards the racecourse. Local schoolchildren, on a day's holiday, swelled the throng of people walking south, hoping for a good vantage point.

After WWI, a revival was needed and this came with the arrival of the Prince of Wales. The first time he competed against professional jockeys was in the Melton Hunt Open Steeplechase. He rode Kinlark, coming fourth behind Culprit, ridden by Capt. Bennet, the winner of the 1923 Grand National. Pressure from his family, concerned about the number of falls he had, obliged the heir to the throne to abandon his equestrian activities and all his horses, apart from one old one, were sold off in 1929.

Nowadays the end of season races are held at Garthorpe, five miles south east of Melton. The racecourse is managed by the Melton Hunt Club, founded in 1955, and is widely recognised as the premier point-to-point course in the country.

The Racecourse

GARTHORPE

The top of Burrough Hill, almost 700 feet above sea level, provides commanding views of the countryside. It is small wonder then that the local Iron Age tribe, over 2000 years ago, chose this site for their hill fort. The great ramparts, with their defensive ditches, enclosing around 5 hectares, have been eroded over time but still make the outline of the hill readily recognisable. In medieval times, the village at its foot was known as Erdburgh, meaning 'the fortress made of earth'.

John Leland, the celebrated 16th century antiquarian, was fascinated by 'Borowe hills', which he visited in 1540, saying that they stand *'in the very highway betwixt Melton and London'.* He noticed stone walls at the entrance and, on digging, found lime cement between the stones. He also remarks that *'very often Roman coins of gold, silver and bronze have been found during ploughing'.*

The flat summit of the hill and the surrounding ramparts make a perfect amphitheatre, and Leland tells us: *'every Monday after White Sunday, com people of the country thereabouts, and shoote, runne, wrestle, dance, and use other feats of like exercise'.* These festivities were replaced eventually by races established by the gentlemen of the Melton Hunt.

In 1921, the young Prince of Wales, the future Edward VIII, lost his two favourite briar-pipes whilst riding in a point-to-point on Burrough Hill. Following a public announcement, volunteers combed the countryside and recovered the pipes for the Royal visitor.

It was, however, at nearby Burrough Court that the course of British history was changed on 10th January 1931. The house was occupied by Viscount Furness and his young American wife, Thelma, who had a very close relationship with the Prince of Wales. The Prince had been invited to a weekend party and Thelma's sister and her husband were to be chaperons. At the last moment the sister was called away but arranged for Mr and Mrs Ernest Simpson to attend in her place. Thus it was that the future King Edward VIII first met Wallis Simpson, the woman for whom he was to give up his throne.

Burrough Hill

BURROUGH-ON-THE-HILL

It is generally agreed that St. Luke's Church, Gaddesby is amongst the best of village churches in Leicestershire. Possibly it was well endowed by the Knights Templar, the lords of the manor, but most of the riotous decoration at the western end of the south aisle seems to date from after their dissolution in 1312. Strange faces stare down at you from every nook and cranny of this unique limestone façade.

Inside, the church seems to have escaped Victorian restoration and even the ancient oak pews have survived from medieval times. From the rafters of the south aisle, a wooden face stares down upon you. All this enhances the special appeal of the church.

However there is one more masterpiece, for in the chancel is an almost life-size marble monument to Colonel Edward Hawkins Cheney C.B., of the Scots Greys. It was not intended for the Parish Church but, with the sale of the Gaddesby estate in 1917, was moved on wooden rollers from the conservatory in nearby Gaddesby Hall.

Edward Cheney joined the Scots Greys as a cornet in 1794 when he was only thirteen years old and immediately saw action fighting Napoleon in the Low Countries. He was severely wounded the next year in Holland but it is his exploits at Waterloo in 1815 that the monument records.

With his commanding officers out of the fray, Cheney led his regiment when Wellington called for the cavalry to charge. He had four horses killed under him and a fifth was injured. The cavalry charges became legendary, as did the deeds of his Sergeant, Charles Ewart, who captured the French standard. Both men were rewarded with medals and promotion.

Joseph Gott, the sculptor, shows Colonel Cheney in the heat of battle astride one of his fallen horses, *Tanner*. In the lower panel, Sergeant Ewart is wresting the French eagle from the enemy. Dragoon and French flags lie at each end of the plinth. It is said that Gott, realising he had left out the horse's tongue, was filled with remorse and committed suicide. There is, however no evidence that Gott died other than from natural causes.

St. Luke's Church

GADDESBY

62

M. WESTON. 09.

Visitors to Long Clawson are often confused by the apparent 'hole' in the middle of the village. This is known to the locals as Castle Field and may be the site of the Saxon settlement belonging to Auti and Ernwy before the Norman Conquest. It has a moated area, house platforms and three medieval fishponds including one across the road in front of the Old Manor House. The first Norman Lord of the Manor, Ivo de Tigervilla, built a new Church here, dedicated to St. Remigius, which he gave to Belvoir Priory.

Ancient churches almost always have surprises and St. Remigius is no exception. High up on the roof of the tower, scratched into the lead, is a drawing of a long vanished windmill. The churchyard also has surprises, not least the headstones depicting the 'Belvoir Angel'. This stylised image of a round-faced angel with curls and outstretched wings is found throughout the Vale and is particularly plentiful at Hickling. The earliest, just 2 feet high, were made of durable Swithland Slate, quarried in the west of the county and were carved between 1690 and 1760. Welsh slate, brought in by canal, soon replaced the local stone; and the larger headstones with a different style have not weathered so well.

In the 18th century, another type of gravestone appeared. It was made of high quality green Charnwood stone and one of the earliest examples is in Clawson Churchyard. Expertly carved by a skilled mason, it records a tragic accident to the son of William Barnes. On 26th June 1781, William Barnes Junior, aged 19, drowned whilst swimming in the village pond, a pastime enjoyed by many of the village youngsters in those days. The gravestone depicts his drowning in exquisite detail, in every way equal to the marble memorials of our more wealthy ancestors.

Not so long ago, there was an inscription over the north door of the church mentioning 'William Barnes, painter' and dated 1777. Possibly this was the same person as the stonemason who left scattered around the Vale many finely carved green slate headstones signed 'Barnes', at the base.

The Belvoir Angel

LONG CLAWSON

M. WESTON 09

Langar airfield straddles the county boundary between Harby and Langar. It was built in 1940 and the concrete runways are said to cover the site of the church of St Ethelburga, a place of pilgrimage in medieval times. Harby windmill, one of the tallest in Leicestershire, was in the direct line of approach and its tower was reduced to a four-storey stump.

The airfield was intended for use by heavy bombers and in 1942 RAF Bomber Command 207 Squadron moved in with their Lancasters. They undertook a total of 149 operations out of Langar but sadly lost 247 crewmen in action; three ground crew also died.

It was from Langar in September 1943 that the BBC brought to the nation a first-hand account of a Lancaster bombing raid on Berlin. This historic recording by Wynford Vaughan Thomas described everything in graphic detail – the searchlights crossing the sky, the flack from German guns, the silence of the crew as their friends were shot down, the elation when an enemy nightfighter plunged to earth. His final comment was "on returning the gentle bump on the tarmac [at Langar] was the sweetest sound I have ever heard".

Local craftsmen were employed at the A V Roe works on the Harby Road where Lancasters were repaired and serviced. Crewmen frequented the local hostelries and became a part of the community. But the Vale now echoed to the sound of ack-ack guns following the searchlight batteries stationed nearby.

The life of the airfield continued after the Squadron had left. In 1952, as part of the NATO force, the Royal Canadian Airforce was based at Langar. Later, John Deere, a major international company, converted the medical block into a factory. Today the airfield is a popular venue for parachuting.

On the 12th May 1994 a memorial was erected to the men of 207 Bomber Squadron. On it is the Squadron coat of arms, authorised by Edward VIII, a winged lion with the motto *Semper Paratus* – be prepared. The City of Leicester adopted 207 Squadron just before WWII and the standard now hangs in Leicester Cathedral.

207 Bomber Squadron

LANGAR AIRFIELD

The village of Stathern, nestling on the slopes below Belvoir Castle with panoramic views over the Vale, was home to Francis Hacker, the Presbyterian squire of the village. His brothers Rowland and Thomas fought for the Royalist cause. He was extremely rigid in his views and caused the vicar of Stathern to be fined £48 for using the old prayer book in church. As a member of the local Parliamentarian Committee of Militia, he enlisted men and collected taxes. Francis was accused of cowardice on several occasions, but Roundhead publications defended his actions. Having an excellent military record in battle saved his reputation and gained him promotion.

Colonels Hacker, Hercules Huncks and Phayre were responsible for guarding King Charles I during his trial at Westminster and, subsequently, until his execution. The death warrant for the King was addressed to them, instructing them to arrange the execution. However, late in the proceedings it was realised that an order to the executioner was also required. Cromwell asked Huncks to write one but this he refused to do. Cromwell himself undertook the task but Huncks still refused to sign. Hacker, however, did sign and this was to lead directly to his own execution eleven years later. Then, at about two o'clock on 30th January 1649, he escorted the King to the scaffold.

The restoration of the monarchy in 1660 was conditional on the granting of pardons to all except those responsible for the murder of Charles I. The Act of Indemnity and Oblivion was passed to facilitate this but, unfortunately for him, Francis Hacker's name was included in the list of those not to be pardoned. Hercules Huncks denied signing the King's death document and was pardoned. Hacker's plea that he was only carrying out orders was not accepted and he was sentenced to death. This meant for the regicides that they would be hanged, drawn and quartered. Uniquely, Hacker was spared this horrific punishment. He was hanged on 19th October 1660 and his body handed over to his family. Tradition has it that he was buried at Stathern. Samuel Pepys' diary notes Hacker's execution, which he missed by turning up on the wrong day.

Stathern from Mill Hill

STATHERN

68

M.WESTON. 09.

Scalford is a pleasant, compact village with many mellow ironstone buildings. It is watched over by its towering parish church, which is dedicated uniquely to Egelwin the Martyr, an obscure Anglo-Saxon Saint.

Its most notorious inhabitant was, perhaps, William Brown, nicknamed Peppermint Billy. William was a habitual criminal, having been convicted in 1837, 1840 and 1843. On the last occasion, he was sentenced to penal transportation to Van Dieman's Land (Tasmania) for a period of ten years. Two of his brothers were also transported, both for horse stealing. What made William unusual was that he returned to England on completion of his sentence. He vowed to have revenge on his accusers.

On 19th June 1856, Alfred Routen, a baker from Asfordby, arrived at the Thorpe toll-bar around twenty to four in the morning. Unable to rouse anyone, he went to the toll-house only to discover a gruesome scene inside. The gatekeeper, Edward Woodcock, aged 70, lay in a pool of blood with knife and gunshot wounds and his young grandson, James, lay dead with his throat cut and all but decapitated. A pistol lay on the ground nearby, together with a distinctive tobacco stopper.

Suspicion turned on William Brown who had been living in a nearby hovel and had disappeared. By chance, a constable from Scalford, whilst pursuing a chicken, found pieces of ripped up clothing in a ditch. Although they had been washed recently, they still had traces of blood on them. The clothes were later identified as belonging to Peppermint Billy as were the pistol and the tobacco stopper. A huge country-wide manhunt ensued and three days later, Brown was recognised and arrested in Wetherby, Yorkshire, and brought back to Leicester by the Chief Constable.

Brown was sent to Leicester Assizes where he was found guilty of murder and Lord Chief Justice Jervis passed the death sentence on him. Peppermint Billy was hanged outside Leicester Prison on Friday 7th August in front of a huge crowd of eager onlookers. It was the last public execution to be held in Leicester; future executions took place inside the prison walls.

Peppermint Billy

SCALFORD

M. WESTON 09

The 70 yards high steeple shows the way to Bottesford parish church, known locally as 'Lady of the Vale'. There is a pleasant churchyard with a stream to one side but St Mary's claim to fame lies in the chancel, which is literally full of elaborate tombs and memorials to the Lords of Belvoir Castle. The earliest were moved from Belvoir Priory at the Dissolution and there is a complete run from the first to the eighth Earls of Rutland. The erection of a mausoleum in the grounds of Belvoir Castle in 1826 brought a timely end to the burials at Bottesford.

The most celebrated, and indeed the finest, tomb is that of the sixth Earl, Francis who died in 1632. The memorial shows the Earl, his wives Frances and Cecilia, and his children Katherine, Henry and Francis. The boys hold skulls to indicate their deaths in infancy and the inscription tells us *'both dyed in their infancy by wicked practise & sorcerye'*.

Amongst the locals working at Belvoir Castle were Joan Flower and her two daughters, Margaret and Philippa. Margaret, responsible for the washhouse, was a resident and the other two women were daily cleaners. Margaret was discovered stealing provisions and was dismissed with a generous gift of forty shillings from the Countess.

The Earl's son, Henry, died and was buried at Bottesford on 23 September 1613. A few years passed before the Flower family was suspected of involvement in the child's death. Joan was described as *'a monstrous malicious woman … her eyes were fiery and hollow, her demeanour strange and exoticke'*. Neighbours told of the women talking to cats, and, apparently, they had cast a spell using a stolen glove belonging to Henry. They were also thought responsible for strange illnesses afflicting the Earl and his family.

The three women were taken to Lincoln for examination. On the way there, Joan requested some bread and butter. Swearing she would choke on it if she were guilty; she fell down dead *'with a horrible excruciation of soule and body'*. The daughters confessed, were *'conuicted of Murther'* and hanged on 11 March 1618/9.

The Witchcraft Tomb

BOTTESFORD

M WESTON '09

A Melton Miscellany

The Mowbrays – Lords of the Manor

Lands, including Melton Mowbray, were held in several counties by the Saxon, Leuric son of Lewin, who was dispossessed after the Battle of Hastings in 1066. Geoffrey de La Guerche (anglicised, de Wirce) with his kinsman Roger de Molbrai had fought alongside William I and continued to be the King's close advisor. He was rewarded with Saxon estates in addition to his lands in Normandy. He married Alveva, a Saxon heiress and niece of Earl Leofric and Lady Godiva of Coventry. On his death around 1088, the estates reverted to the Crown and were passed to his nephew Robert de Mowbray, Earl of Northumberland and lord of the manor of Melton.

Robert was imprisoned for treason in 1096 after a failed revolt against William II. He was forced, by Papal decree, to divorce his wife, Matilda d'Aquilla. When Henry I appointed Nigel de Albini, a relation of Robert, fourth lord of Melton in 1101, he had been a landless son of a minor Baron and was one of Henry's 'new men'. The King gave him the lands of Geoffrey de Wirce and Matilda, the divorced wife of Robert de Mowbray. Later, Nigel divorced Matilda and married

75

Gundreda de Gornay, also a relation of the Mowbray family.

Their eldest son, Roger, was a teenager when, by royal decree, he took the name of Mowbray and inherited his father's estates. On returning from the Crusades, he became a generous benefactor, contributed to the building of St. Mary's Parish Church and a priory at Kirby Bellars for his brother, Hamo. He granted land at Burton, later Burton Lazars that became the headquarters of the crusading Order of the Knights of St. Lazarus in England. The earthworks are under the custodianship of the farmer, Mr Geoff Child. The western gatehouse, located close to the old London road, was the entrance for nobility and royalty who partook of the Master's hospitality. Leland reported a *'fine collegiate Church'* here just before Henry VIII dissolved the Order.

William de Mowbray was one of the Barons who signed the Magna Carta in 1216. The seventh seal shows the Lion Rampant of the Mowbray's, now used by Melton Borough. Three generations later, in 1267, Roger became a peer and *'lord of Melton'*. The earliest reference to the town as Melton Mowbray occurs in 1282.

In 1399, Thomas de Mowbray, an acclaimed parliamentary orator, was created Duke of Norfolk and immortalised in Shakespeare's *Richard II*. John, the last Mowbray lord of Melton died in 1475, leaving his young daughter as heir. She was betrothed to Richard of York, one of the two princes supposedly murdered in the Tower of London. The Mowbray ties with Melton ended and the estates were divided between their close relatives, the Howards and the Berkeleys. The Howards became Dukes of Norfolk and the Berkeleys held the manor of Melton until the late 1500s.

The Barony of Mowbray lay in abeyance until, on 11th January 1878, an announcement appeared in the *London Gazette*. Queen Victoria had summoned *'under the Great Seal'* Alfred Joseph, Baron Stourton (Wiltshire) to assume the full title of Lord Mowbray, Seagrave and Stourton, *'he being one of the heirs of Roger de Mowbray, who was summoned to Parliament in the 11th year of the reign of Edward 1st'*.

THE GRAND ALL ENGLAND CRICKET MATCH

The origins of cricket are lost in time. *Wisden,* the cricketers' bible, suggests somewhere between the Romans and the Norman Conquest. A medieval illustration in the Bodleian Library, Oxford, shows monks playing a game, wielding a bat above their tonsured heads. The game was well established by Tudor times but it was not until 1744 that the earliest known Laws of Cricket were drawn up. Coincidentally, it was in this year that cricket was first recorded in Leicestershire.

Early cricket matches were invariably played for money and the sums wagered could be enormous, hence the need for Laws. Arguments between teams were common. In 1781, the first match between Leicester and Nottingham was abandoned as a draw when a dispute arose which simmered on for the next fifty years. The gentlemen of Melton agreed to a return match with the gentlemen of Cossington, only if they would take the umpire's decision as final!

From 1846, the All-England XI started touring and in about 1855 it was the turn of Melton Mowbray to act as hosts. The venue was on the eastern edge of town, beyond the new Workhouse in a paddock off Southern Lane, which is now Saxby Road. The visitors easily beat the Melton and District XXII by an innings and 30 runs, a result that was probably expected. Not learning from this setback, Melton was similarly beaten two years later.

The third match was played over three days from 13th June 1872. This time, the Melton team took the precaution of recruiting three outsiders. These were Dr W. G. Grace, the greatest cricketer who ever lived, his brother, G. F., and J. Lillywhite, probably the player who was to captain England in the first ever two Tests. Anticipation and excitement reached fever pitch with a carnival atmosphere around the town. Tradesmen closed their stores, not wishing to miss the action.

For the comfort of visitors, three booths, run by Messrs. Dale, Goodacre and Sturgess supplied refreshments, whilst separate tents were provided for the ladies and for the players and committee. The Band of the Third Leicestershire Rifle Volunteers was on hand to entertain the crowds.

Fine weather attracted over 4,000 spectators every day. The wicket was said to be tolerable, although an occasional ball rose up in an alarming manner. Needless to say, W. G. was the top scorer for Melton in both innings. At two o'clock on the third day the All-England XI needed 162 runs to win. W. G. was soon amongst the wickets when the teams adjourned for dinner. The match ended at 5 pm but not before W. G. had taken over as wicket keeper, Lillywhite had made a magnificent one-handed catch and G. F. had clean bowled the last two batsmen without scoring. Melton achieved a great victory by 92 runs.

The match report, printed by M. A. Whalley of King Street, concluded *'the whole of the proceedings were characterised by the total absence of anything inconsistent with order and harmony, all parties doing their utmost to make the affair a complete success'.*

In memory of these matches, the field is still known as the 'All England Sports Ground' and is owned by the Town Estate on behalf of the town's inhabitants.

VISCOUNT MELBOURNE AND THE PLAY CLOSE RIOTS

By the beginning of the nineteenth century, the Town Estate was in possession of much run down and dilapidated property. It was decided that this should be sold and an Act of Parliament enabling it to do so was passed in 1826. This started a period of regeneration that gathered momentum. A land dispute then arose involving the northern part of Play Close between Waverley House and the churchyard. The close was owned by William Lamb, Viscount Melbourne, paternal mentor to the young Queen Victoria, and lord of the manor of Melton. Over many years, it had been used to hold fairs, sports and games and it was considered by the inhabitants of the town to be common land.

Mr Beaumont, from the bakehouse in Church Lane, had built and rented out a number of pig styes, barns, cowsheds and garden plots, encroaching onto the Play Close. The townsfolk considered them to be not only eyesores, but also a deliberate attempt to deprive them of their rights. By 1848, hostility had grown, culminating in the deliberate vandalism to the buildings and destruction of the gardens. Special constables were called out to quell the riot. People were arrested and taken to the King Street lock-up. Later they were fined at the Leicester Sessions. Soon after, a satirical text appeared entitled *'A laughable Farce of Peelers and Specials catching National Guards'*. Published by a private soldier, it included the actual names of those involved.

In the Town Warden's accounts of the time is an entry which reads *'To Mr John Towne, Mr Gray and others, for a journey to London, and other costs, on account of the Play Close Riots, £10-3s-7d'*. The purpose was to visit Lord Melbourne, now an elderly man, but little progress was made.

The Town Estate was forced to act again after similar riots occurred the following year on a holiday featuring a firework display in the Market Place. A group of young men uprooted trees, turned a horse loose and generally ran riot. By now, Viscount Melbourne had died and the Town Estate was able to purchase the manorial rights for £650. There was insufficient money to buy the Play Close and Messrs. T. Ward and W. T. Tuxford bought it for £170, agreeing to sell it to the Town Estate at a later date. In the event, this did not happen until 1866. It was the first time the feoffees had been responsible for a recreation ground. Today, it remains open parkland, available to all, at the very centre of Town.

THE HEAVYWEIGHT BOXING CHAMPION OF THE WORLD

On the afternoon of Saturday 28th September 1811, the streets of Melton Mowbray were surprisingly empty as were the villages for miles around. Some 20,000 people descended on a field in the parish of Wymondham, east of the town, for the biggest sporting event many local villagers had ever seen.

They had come for the defence of the heavyweight boxing

championship of the world between Englishman and holder, Tom Cribb, and the black American ex-slave, Thomas Molyneux. Cribb, aged 30, had beaten Molyneux over 35 rounds the previous year but the outcome of these contests was unpredictable. Bare-knuckle fights were not regulated and continued until one of the contestants could no longer fight. Bouts were known to last up to 100 rounds. The Marquis of Queensberry rules were not adopted for another 56 years.

The contest was illegal, but the organisers had chosen the field well. It was on the borders of Leicestershire, Rutland and Lincolnshire and a slight change of location could evade any interference from the law. It was academic, since the presence of such a large crowd could not be kept secret and magistrates from Rutland and, no doubt elsewhere, had rushed to the fight in their carriages.

Only the farmer, owner of the field, was not pleased. From all directions the crowds had forced their way, wrecking his hedges and damaging trees. He demanded £50 before any fight could take place. The hunting gentry had no cash and their signatures on cheques were considered untrustworthy. A draper and horse-breeder, member of the Quorn Hunt and a heavyweight himself, George Marriott from Melton Mowbray was the only one the farmer knew and trusted. George's cheque saved the day.

Apart from watching the fight, the gentry were occupied in making wagers and Captain Barclay backed Cribb for £1,000. As the two contestants entered the ring, mounted on a 25ft square wooden platform, the crowds moved in for a better view and men stood on horses at the back.

After 11 rounds lasting 19 minutes and 10 seconds, Molyneux lay unconscious with his jaw clearly broken. Cribb had retained his title and, despite his exhaustion, he danced around the stage in triumph. He eventually retired unbeaten and later became a publican, spending his days relating his fighting exploits to his customers. He died in 1848, aged 67.

The nearby farmhouse was renamed Cribb's Lodge and the field, Cribb's meadow. The Leicestershire and Rutland Trust for Nature Conservation now maintains it for its orchids and butterflies which are specific to this part of the County. Any visitor to this peaceful wildlife haven would find it hard to imagine the scene on that day two hundred years ago.

ALFRED ALLEN AND THE GREAT SIOUX WAR

Alfred Ernest was born on 14th August 1848 to Silas and Mary Allen of Melton Mowbray. He grew up in Chapel Street where his father was a saddler. The times were hard and many families were separated forever as children emigrated in search of a better life. Alfred's elder brother, Walter Brett Allen sailed south on the mission boat, *Dayspring*, working as a cook. He married a ship's maid whilst in the New Hebrides (Vanuatu) and was to settle in Australia.

Alfred chose to go to America, working as a watchmaker in Boston, Massachusetts. Things were about to change however, when on 3rd October 1873 the 25 year old Alfred was enlisted into the US Army by Lieutenant James Ropes. The National Enlistment Register describes him as strong, 5 ft 8 inches tall with brown eyes, black hair and a dark complexion. Alfred, now Private Allen of the 7th Cavalry, was soon to be sent west to the edge of Indian Territory.

Many of the Sioux tribes had signed the Fort Laramie Treaty in 1868 and settled in a reservation between the Missouri River and the west Dakota boundary. One, a Hunkpapa Lakota Sioux holy man by the name of Sitting Bull refused to comply. The discovery of gold in the Black Hills sent a surge of prospectors to the area, encroaching on reservation lands and forcing the Sioux into six smaller areas. In 1876, war broke out and the 7th Cavalry, including Private Allen, entered the fray under the command of Lieutenant Colonel George Armstrong Custer.

On the 25th June 1876, the most famous battle of the Great Sioux War took place near a fork in the Little Bighorn River, Montana. Custer attacked what he believed was a village of 800 people, only to find a great coalition of 3000 warriors led by Sitting Bull and Crazy Horse. The 7th Cavalry were massacred to a man.

Heroic acts were attributed to the 209 men who died that day and Custer's Last Stand was to attain mythological status, later exploited by Hollywood. The awful reality was that the Battle was a complete rout. The dreadful news hit the headlines as America prepared for the 4th July Centennial celebrations of the Declaration of Independence. Friends and relatives of Private Allen received black-edged mourning cards, one of which is preserved at the Melton Carnegie Museum.

On a monument near to the site of the battle is the name, Private Alfred Ernest Allen. Revenge came on 29th December at the Battle of Wounded Knee. A giant statue of Crazy Horse now stares over Sioux territory. Sitting Bull escaped to Canada but surrendered in 1881 and briefly joined Buffalo Bill's Wild West Show. He was shot dead by police in 1890. In 1980, the Sioux were finally awarded financial compensation.

Silas, a widower, committed suicide in the Leicester Union Workhouse on 21st April 1881, aged 63. Walter died in 1910. His Australian descendents had no knowledge of their Great Uncle Alfred until only a few years ago.

THE FIRST MIDNIGHT STEEPLECHASE

From her first visit to Melton Mowbray with her sister Star,

Lady Augusta Fanny Rous fell in love with its hunting and social life. Years later, after returning often with her husband, Cecil Fane, for the winter seasons, she wrote: *'I have never changed my opinion since I first went there that Melton is the one and only place to live.'*

The Fanes were staying at the Old Club in Burton Street when Lady Augusta challenged her dinner party guests from the Bell Hotel, a haunt for Army officers, to hold a moonlight steeplechase on her birthday. Col. Baldock of Craven Lodge agreed to be the starter and judge over a course at the Spinneys, near Thorpe Arnold. Here, Mr Alfred Brocklehurst leased land from Mr Gunby where he schooled his steeplechasers over a 3-mile course. Word soon got out and the race became the talk of the town.

On Monday 10th March 1890, 25 guests sat down to Augusta's 32nd birthday dinner with the men dressed in red evening coats and white breeches. A groom interrupted the dinner, informing the guests that heavy clouds were blocking out the moonlight. Col. Baldock saved the day by borrowing lamps from Mr Beddington, the stationmaster. Willing helpers hung them either side of the fences with one on a tall tree at the halfway mark.

The competitors donned white nightshirts over their red coats and Major Burnaby wore Augusta's frilly pink gossamer nightie. Riders and ladies in pony carts clattered through the streets followed by a procession of horses and carriages. The ladies gathered at the start/finish line where, at 11.30pm, Col. Baldock sounded a horn. After a false start, 11 riders galloped into the darkness with the spectators cheering loudly. The race was out of sight of the crowds until they heard the riders returning with their white shirts bobbing up and down. Two clear leaders emerged heading hell for leather at the last fence. As they jumped together, Count Zborowski was thrown from his horse, Topthorn. He remounted immediately but Burnaby, on Midnight, won the race. As the stragglers came in and people drifted back to town, the full moon shone out over the countryside. Excited voices and the clatter of carriages and horses on the cobbled roads again roused the sleeping residents.

Count Zborowski of Coventry House, who had donated the winner's trophy, had arranged supper when he gallantly presented the prize to Major Burnaby, an ivory 3-handled cup, carved from the base of an elephant's tusk and mounted in silver.

The following Sunday the Rev. Karney remarked on the uproar in the middle of the night using as text for his sermon: *'Have no fellowship with the unfruitful works of darkness but rather reprove them'* (Ephesians 5.11). Karney, unaware that his congregation was doubled up with laughter, added: *"the manly art of horsemanship had been degraded and discredited"*. It was the First Midnight Steeplechase and, like many events of the time, it would soon be immortalised in an engraving.

TEMPLE CROZIER OF COSTON ON THE LONDON STAGE

Temple Edgecombe Crozier was the son of Rev. James Crozier who, in his later years became Rector of Coston, a tiny rural parish about eight miles from Melton. Temple was well educated and apparently, an excellent football player. He was apprenticed to a firm of corn merchants but after only eighteen months he become bored and ran away to join a travelling show, hoping to become an actor.

Temple was described as young, handsome, popular and conscientious. He slowly progressed in his new career, playing juvenile leads in small town productions, and like many before him, he made his way to London. After further minor provincial roles, his big break came in June 1896. Miss V. St. Lawrence had taken over the lease of the failing Novelty Theatre in London's Great Queen Street and greatly changed its fortunes. She decided to form a permanent company and to this end, Temple was recruited as a leading man.

His first night under the bright lights of the London stage was a double bill, starting with a farce, *Ici on parle francais,* in which he played the lead. This was followed by *Sins of the Night,* a melodrama by Frank Harvey where Temple played the villain, Manuel Ramez, opposite his close friend, Wilfred Franks, as the hero, Pablo. The show opened at 8.30pm on Monday 10th August 1896 and just after midnight reached its climax. The fifth and final act ends dramatically when Pablo, seeking revenge for his murdered sister, stabs Ramez with a jewelled stiletto. As Crozier realistically staggered and fell on his back, the audience cheered. He lay there, the knife still in his chest, as the curtain rose to huge applause.

Crozier still lay there as the audience left, his face ashen as his colleagues withdrew the knife. He uttered his last words to his close friend: *"Don't worry, old man, I'm alright"*. Four doctors arrived and pronounced Crozier dead. While Franks was arrested and taken to Bow Street Police Station, Crozier, still in his costume and make up, was left overnight where he fell. The next morning, his body was removed to St. Giles mortuary to await an inquest at Goldsmith's Street. The show went on the next night with new actors in the roles of Ramez and Pablo.

Newspapers all over the country announced the tragedy; indeed, the story appeared as far afield as the *New York Times* and the *Brisbane Courier*. The headline in the *Melton Mowbray Times* on 14th August read *'Terrible Tragedy In A London Theatre – Coston Gentleman Fatally Injured.'*

In Melton Mowbray, Superintendent Bolt, on receiving a telegram, asked Rev. Crozier to attend the inquest. The jury returned a verdict of death by misadventure and condemned the use of real weapons on the stage. In view of this, all charges against Wilfred Franks were dropped.

Crozier's body was brought by rail from St. Pancras to Saxby Station east of Melton. From there, the cortege made its way to Coston Church to lie overnight before the funeral. On Sunday 16th August, the little church was packed. Staff and actors of the Novelty Theatre Company joined the local congregation for the funeral service. The Lyric Theatre donated £5 to a fund for a memorial plaque to be placed near the altar in Coston Church. It describes Temple Crozier as a *faithful friend and a thorough worker'* who was *'held in high esteem'.*

Melton Mowbray, the Metropolis of Hunting

An early history of hunting as a sport was that by Gaston Phoebus, Count of Foix, in 1387. A soldier by trade, he declared that all his life he had delighted in *'arms, love and hunting'*. Hunting was the sport of royalty, nobility and bishops. Archbishop de Melton, a 14th century Rector of St. Mary's Church, expected to hunt when visiting religious houses, at great expense to his hosts.

Melton was still a small village little changed over the centuries when the Lambton brothers from Durham first came in 1787, renting a house in Sherrard Street for six seasons. The quiet town lacked the bawdy social life of those nearby.

Nimrod, the pen-name of Charles Apperley, visited Melton at this time and described it as an insignificant little town prettily situated in a rich vale with nothing of note except St. Mary's Church.

Almost overnight, Melton was forced to accommodate the increasing number of gentlemen staying for the winter. Town houses replaced run down properties and new stables were built to house up to 40 hunters required by each gentleman in a season. Before the railways, coaches brought the visitors along the rough country roads. In 1809, the mail coach from Leeds to London began running through Melton. Leaving

London at 8 am, it reached the George Hotel in High Street at 2.30 pm the next day.

Melton became the 'metropolis of hunting' for European royalty, nobility and politicians. It was ideally placed at the junction of the territories of the Belvoir, Quorn and Cottesmore Hunts which converging at the Market Place, each located in perfect hunting countryside. A gentleman could hunt with three different packs for 6 days in a week and rest on Sunday.

Many of the upper floors in the town centre were let to bachelors. Gentleman's clubs opened where French or London chefs were employed and the evenings were spent dining and drinking and endlessly discussing the day's run. The Old Club in Burton Street was the first, followed by Lord Alveney's Club in High Street and Lord Rokeby's Club at Coventry House.

Mr Beeby in Burton Street was one of several horse dealers in the town and Mr Heap in King Street provided enough fine wines and clarets to last a season. Saddlers and drapers to the gentry moved into town. Mr Marriott in the Market Place went hunting in a blue coat to advertise his wares. Local participants included farmers and clergymen, the flying parsons, who rebuilt or extended their houses and added stables. Other pastimes had to be accommodated. Pigeon shooting was organised by Mr Webster and the venue for cockfighting was the rear garden of the Anne of Cleves House, where a sunken amphitheatre held up to 500 'punters'.

Until the 1850s, few ladies accompanied their husbands. The requirement for another 20 horses and the extra household staff was considered too high a price in return for relinquishing the 'bachelor high life'.

The Harborough, the Bell and the George Hotels were soon booked up years in advance. Visitors could spend as much as 50,000 shillings in a season. Architects were in demand and a regeneration and expansion of the town began. Hunting boxes surrounded by landscaped grounds were built outside the old medieval boundaries and, soon new 'villa' developments were to be found along the roads out of town.

Much of Melton's heritage has been lost. Elgin Lodge, Dorian Lodge, Newport Lodge, North Lodge, Mowbray Lodge and Six Elms have all gone. In Sherard Street, The Elms was home to the Norman family and the Duke of Portland spent 'the best years of his life' at the Limes. Woodlands and the Warwick Lodge stables have both suffered recent fires. The following gives a necessarily brief flavour of a fast disappearing aspect of our history which, like it or not, was to shape the town that we see today.

Town Houses: The Jersey Lily

The Frewin family from Cold Overton Hall were important

landowners. Charles Frewin bought the Melton manor house on the corner of Burton Street and Mill Street. R. W. Johnson, a Melton architect, designed a new house with stables to the rear and the tender stipulated a completion date within 3 months. The old Manor House of Lord Melbourne, built in 1770, was demolished and Charles Frewin moved into his new house in 1870, £2245 lighter in pocket. Today, the house is just one of several important buildings in the town designed by the architect.

On the corner of Wilton Place and High Street was a grand town house which welcomed a glamorous woman who charmed nobility and royalty from all over Europe. Emillie Charlotte le Breton was born and grew up in Jersey, the daughter of the Rev. William Corbet de Breton. In 1874, at the age of twenty, she married Edward Langtry, whose main attraction was that he owned a yacht. She was noticed by the painter Millais whose portrait of her holding a lily set her on the road to fame. She was the essential guest at any social occasion and was to be a pioneer of celebrity endorsement for such things as soap and cosmetics.

Lily captured the heart of Moreton Frewin. Their first meeting was a disaster. At a party given by Lady Manners, the Duchess of Rutland, at Belvoir Castle, Frewin arrived late and flustered and, having been introduced to Lily, he could only murmur trivialities and gaze at her beauty. However, it was Frewin who attracted Lily to Melton. It was as mistress to Albert Edward, Prince of Wales, later Edward VII that Lily is best remembered for. The Prince had a lovenest built for them in Bournemouth, where he was a frequent visitor.

Frewin was heartbroken, decided to sell off his hunters and emigrate to Wyoming in 1878. As a parting gift, Frewin gave Lily his favourite hunter, Redskin. He wrote: *I found it impossible to compete with Prince Rudolph, much less the Prince of Wales, but I had the joy of seeing her riding my horse when out exercising with HRH'.*

Lily's affair with the Prince of Wales lasted only three years until she misbehaved at a party and Bertie's attention was caught by the actress Sarah Bernhardt. By now, the Langtrys were virtually penniless and Lilly turned to acting. Her first stage performance was in *She Stoops to Conquer* at the Haymarket Theatre. She went to America, where she divorced her husband, and was a great success on the stage. Lily Langtry married the wealthy Sir Hugo de Bathe in 1899, continuing to lead the hectic social life of the 1920s until she died in Monte Carlo in 1929.

The Harborough Hotel and the Empress of Austria

The Harborough Hotel in Burton Street, near the railway station, was entered through a wide arch leading to the stables at the rear. In September 1874, Mr Dale, the proprietor, and

Frank Gilliard, huntsman to the Duke of Rutland's hounds, received telegrams which would upset their plans. HRH Elizabeth, Empress of Austria, who expected everything to be organised, however short the notice, would be arriving that evening. Having married Franz Joseph, the Emperor, at the age of 16, the rigid protocol of her husband's life did not suit her light-hearted personality. She escaped by travelling around Europe enjoying the hunting.

At the Harborough, Mr Dale had to prepare rooms for a retinue of 17 including a Grand Duke and a Count, with their hunters. Guests were rapidly moved to the George and Bell Hotels.

Gilliard's telegram, requesting a change of fixture from the Lincolnshire side of Belvoir country, chose a site at Three Queens near Melton. Elizabeth, described by a contemporary as *'the most beautiful horsewoman that ever lived'*, was immaculately turned out with a tall hat, three pairs of white gloves to protect her hands and a fan to protect her face from the elements. Her greatest worry was of scratching her face when jumping hedges, so Count Botazzi warned Gilliard to mind where he led the riders.

The Empress rode with good style and, after being presented with the 'brush', the party toured the kennels and stables at Belvoir. With the Duke away, Gilliard and his wife entertained the Empress and her party at luncheon. On their return to Melton they visited the Earl of Wilton and other acquaintances before they wearily took their seats on the evening train to London. The ousted guests returned to the Harborough Hotel.

Gilliard had impressed the Empress and was commissioned to buy a pack of the best beagles, money no object. Over the summer, he assembled 12 couples of the famous Belvoir tan hounds and hunted with them. He personally delivered the hounds to Austria where he stayed for a week as a guest of the Empress.

The Empress, known as Sissi, and her family met many tragedies in later life. Her son, Archduke Rudolf, died in a suicide pact with his mistress. Elizabeth, who wished to die in a hunting accident, was fatally stabbed by an anarchist in Geneva in 1889. Her nephew and husband's surviving heir, Franz Ferdinand, was assassinated at Sarajevo in 1914. This last tragedy signalled the start of the 1st World War.

WYNDHAM LODGE

The Lodge, at the junction of Burton Road and Ankle Hill and named after Colonel Charles Wyndham, enjoys extensive views over the town. The surrounding woodland covers the steep slope down to the banks of the River Eye. From the Town, only the chimneys of the Lodge can be seen above the woods.

Charles Wyndham, second son of the third Earl of Egremont, served in the Peninsular War as a Major in the Scots Greys. Promoted to Colonel, he fought in the Battle of Waterloo. King George IV described this powerful soldier as *'the hand-somest man in the army'*. With his family he moved to Hill House in 1840 and built stabling and a comfortable hunting lodge close to Melton Mowbray. A heavyweight of 20 stone, he became a familiar and well-loved figure by the Hunts and the townsfolk. Huntsmen, faced with an impenetrable hedge, inevitably shouted "Where's Wyndham?" and the Colonel would barge through the obstacle leaving a gap for the rest of the field.

Charles also donated generously to the repairs to the Parish Church. When Dr Colles organised a special fund-raising service, Colonel Wyndham and members of the Hunt 'guard-ed' the doors, collecting contributions. The memorial window in the north transept of St. Mary's Church, written in Latin, records his career and generosity to the people of Melton.

In 1852, Charles Wyndham was promoted to General. He left Melton to take up his new post of Governor of the Tower of London. In 1869, a new lodge was built on the same site, but the name of Wyndham was retained. Whilst Mr Chaplin lived here, part of the land to the west was sold to Lord Hamilton for a new lodge.

After the First World War, Col. Dalgleish bought Wyndham Lodge and gave it to the people of Melton as a War Memorial Hospital with a trust fund to ensure its future upkeep. A recently built new hospital has led to the sale of Wyndham Lodge for redevelopment.

CRAVEN LODGE AND THE ROYAL APARTMENTS

Burton House, on the hillside south of the River Eye, was built for Dr Keal in about 1827. The Hon. W. G. Craven, nephew of the 1st Earl of Craven, bought and converted it into a large hunting lodge in the 1850's. His wife, Mary Catherine Yorke, daughter of Earl Hardwicke, was a great beauty whose close friend was Princess Mary Adelaide. Craven Cottage became the social hub of the town but, after around eight years with their marriage failing, the Cravens left. There then followed a succession of owners, which included William Younger, the Edinburgh brewer.

After the First World War, Captain Michael Wardell let out apartments in the Lodge, charging bachelors 10 guineas a week for board and lodging. This became the most luxurious hunting club in Melton with stabling for 62 hunters and 10 saddle rooms.

The Prince of Wales, Prince Henry and Prince George were

regular visitors to the Craven Club and, in 1923, the Prince of Wales stayed longer. He enjoyed his visits to Melton and the Urban District Council passed plans for his private residential quarters attached to the Lodge. The new annex was built with its own stabling, identified by the Prince of Wales feathers. Surprisingly, the stairwell was left unplastered and the rooms were sparsely furnished. The Prince spent much of his leisure time in his 'second home', as he liked to call it.

The Prince of Wales, Duke of Gloucester, Prince George and numerous Lords and Ladies attended the Embassy Dance Club above the shops on the corner of King Street and Market Place. By 1929, HRH the Duke of York, the future King George VI, also secured apartments and stables at Craven Lodge where the King's third son, the Duke of Gloucester stayed for the hunting. The Duke of Kent appeared on the Melton hunting scene in 1927 when a Poker and Dance Party was held in celebration. The Duke of Gloucester had new stables built off Hamilton Drive. By now the Royal brothers were inseparable on the hunting field.

For a decade, Craven Lodge functioned as the hunting residence for the Royal family and their close friends. The national press rated the weekend dances as brilliant as anything in London. The three Princes maintained an interest in Town life, joining with the public at charity dances and the Farmer's Union dinners at the Corn Exchange. In February 1929, ow-ing to the state of health of King George V, the Prince of Wales ceased hunting to concentrate on affairs of State. On his last day he visited the stables and said goodbye to his magnificent hunters before they were sold.

The army requisitioned the Lodge during the Second World War, and afterwards an attempt to re-establish the Club failed. It was bought by the County Council and became a residential school. In 2006, it was sold for £1.27 million and now awaits its fate. Its name maintains the connections with the Craven family and the apartments, specifically built for the Prince of Wales, are a lasting legacy of Melton's close association with the Royal family.

WARWICK LODGE

In the late 1800s, Melton was still relatively undeveloped south of the River Eye. This was an area of green fields and spinneys interspersed with grand hunting lodges, imposing stable blocks and formal gardens. The last of the large hunting boxes to be built, in 1902, was Hamilton Lodge, named after Gavin, 2nd Lord Hamilton of Dalzell. He was a staunch Liberal, and served as Lord-in-Waiting (government whip in the House of Lords), to both Edward VII and King George V. A particular feature of the lodge was the oak panelling, made from timber from Hamilton's Scottish estates. Alongside the house, a two-storey stable block was built around three sides of a large courtyard in the same style as the lodge and equally imposing.

Frances, Countess of Warwick, a noted society beauty, took over and re-named the Lodge. She was universally known as 'Daisy' and was the inspiration of the song *Daisy, Daisy*. She had many affairs, most notably with the future Edward VII, who sent her countless letters, addressing the Countess as 'Dear Daisy'. On her marriage, Frances became Lady Brooke and probably not all of her children were her husband's. Unlike most of the society ladies, she was quite unable to be discreet and she became known as the 'Babbling Brooke'. She attempted, unsuccessfully, to blackmail King George V by threatening to publish his father's love letters. Unusually for her time, the Countess became a socialist and stood for Parliament as a Labour candidate. However, she only succeeded in alienating the voters with her extravagant furs and pearls. Daisy was also a lover of animals and everywhere she stayed, the house would be over-run with dogs. Monkeys let loose around the house would leap up curtains, walk along picture rails and land on the shoulders of visitors, much to their alarm.

A later resident, Ambrose Clarke, recognised the talent of John Ferneley and returned to America with many paintings purchased during his stay. The lodge was later purchased by Captain Edward Brook who lent it to the Duke and Duchess of Gloucester for the 1935 hunting season.

Warwick Lodge saw a drastic change in fortunes during the War. It was established as a residential nursery for about 40 homeless and orphaned children, many of them refugees from the London blitz. In 1955, the Melton and Belvoir Urban District Council bought the property to use as offices and the grand, panelled hall became the Council Chamber. The lodge has been vacant recently and the stable block has been damaged by fire.

THE LODGE, DALBY ROAD

The Lodge on Dalby Road became home to Sir Francis Grant who was much acclaimed as an artist. Born in Edinburgh in 1803, the fourth son of Francis Grant of Kilbraston House in Perthshire, the young man was described by Sir Walter Scott in his diary for 26 March 1831 as *'passionately fond of fox hunting and other sports. He had a strong passion for painting and made a little collection. [He felt] that a younger brother's fortune would not last long under the expenses of a good stud.'* Scott added that Francis did not warm to the thought of joining the legal profession and he *'is not going to be content with sitting at the bottom of his father's table and passing the claret'*. In the early 1820's Francis, accompanied his two elder brothers to Melton, and stayed at the Thistle Club in High Street, run by Capt. Ross. Local artist John Ferneley, who painted the three brothers mounted on their hunters in 1823, gave him encouragement. Grant married Isabella, third daughter of Lady Elizabeth (née Manners) and Richard Norman.

Grant rapidly gained a reputation for his paintings. At the age of 31, his first exhibits at the Royal Academy included the well known *Melton Breakfast,* painted at the Old Club in Burton Street. The Duke of Rutland has a second version, painted for Mr Little Gilmour. By 1840, his Royal Academy painting of Queen Victoria riding with Lord Melbourne in Windsor Park made him the most fashionable portrait painter of the day. He was described by a lady at the Court of Queen Victoria *'as the handsomest man, and the most gifted artist in the Kingdom'.*

It was after this exhibit that Grant bought the Lodge in Dalby Road where he lived for the next 40 years although he still kept his London home, Sussex Villa, in Regent's Park. In 1866, he was elected President of the Royal Academy and was knighted shortly afterwards.

In his latter years, Grant leased the Lodge to many notable tenants. James Gordon Bennett Jr and his sister, amongst the first Americans to come to Melton for the sporting season, rented it in 1877. Bennett's 14 horses, stabled at the George Hotel, had increased to 25 by the end of the season. His father, a Scotsman, had emigrated to America and, by 1835, had established the pioneering *New York Herald.*

Bennett Junior, born in New York in 1841, took over as editor and was to send Henry Morton Stanley to Africa to find David Livingstone in 1871. Stanley, born John Richards in Wales, was abandoned in the workhouse as a child, worked his passage on a ship to New Orleans, where he adopted his foster parent's name. On finding David Livingstone in Tanganyika, Stanley is reported to have said the famous words "Dr Livingstone, I presume".

After Stanley had completed another expedition to trace the Congo River funded jointly by the *Daily Telegraph,* he came to recuperate at the Lodge with his editor and dined with his host and Edward Lawson of the *Telegraph.* Stanley never forgot his British roots despite gaining US citizenship in 1885. In 1890 he returned, was re-naturalised and was later knighted.

Bennett's stay was his first and last visit to Melton Mowbray, which he is reputed to have described as a "lunatic asylum in pink coats!" He acquired a reputation for harebrained schemes and dangerous stunts. When he flew a small, wooden stunt-plane low and fast through an open-ended barn, wood flew in all directions, the plane emerged wingless, but Bennett lived to tell the tale. An amazed reporter is said to have exclaimed: "It's Gordon Bennett!", which became a household expression.

On the 5th October 1878, Sir Francis Grant died suddenly from a heart attack. His family honoured his wishes and declined a burial in Westminster Abbey. The funeral, conducted by Dr Thompson, Archbishop of York, took place at Melton Mowbray. Amongst the pallbearers were the Duke of Rutland, the Marquis of Bristol, Viscount Hardinge and Lord Kinnaird with 300 members of the Royal Academy in the funeral cortege. He was laid to rest in the King Street cemetery, now St. Mary's Close. Of the once imposing memorial, the headstone survives and, in St. Mary's Church, there is a memorial window. The following year, a sale included a portrait of Sir Walter Scott and Joshua Reynolds 'sitters chair', now in the possession of the Royal Academy. Lady Grant and their daughter remained in Melton until her death in 1893. In 1932, the Lodge was sold, re-named Dorian Lodge and eventually turned into flats.

John Ferneley of Elgin Lodge, Artist

In country houses, a display of family portraits was a requirement. The country squire also hired artists to paint the prize-winning bull or the favourite stallion. By the nineteenth century, as Melton grew into a hunting centre, artists were in great demand. Miniature artists were also attracted here as the new fashion for carrying a portrait of a loved one became more popular. Henry Alken became famous for recording the different facets of the hunt and incidents such as 'Painting the Town Red'.

John Ferneley was a Leicestershire man, born in Thrussington in 1782. He was working as an apprentice wheelwright to his father, when the fifth Duke of Rutland noticed his paintings on the sides of the wooden wagons. Ferneley, encouraged by the Duke, studied for 3 years under Benjamin Marshall in London. He became quite a successful artist and in 1814 returned to Melton where he built Elgin Lodge, named after the Elgin marbles much admired by him, off the Scalford Road where he made his studio.

Ferneley became a respected sporting artist to the gentry whose long and prolific career lasted nearly 50 years. He exhibited at the Royal Academy and major exhibitions. Throughout this time, his fees remained unchanged, ranging from 10 guineas for painting a horse to 100 guineas for a large group. His paintings of hunt meets are now much sought after. His sons, Claude Lorraine and John Junior, continue their father's profession.

John died in 1860 and is buried in his home village of Thrussington. Elgin Lodge was demolished in 1982 after a terrible fire. Later, archaeologists working on the site found quantities of small glass globules, the melted remnants of chandeliers.

Sir Francis Burdett of Kirby Park

The Quorn Hunt is probably the most famous Hunt in the world and claims an ancestry going back to 1696 when it was founded by Mr Thomas Boothby, or 1753 by Hugo Meynell, depending on the historian. It is now based in the village of Kirby Bellars, just to the west of Melton Mowbray. Kirby

Gate, so called after a tollgate, is on the east side of the village, on the main Melton to Leicester Road, where traditionally, the opening meet of the season is held.

Nearby is the old manor house, Kirby Park, with a stone facade, five coped gables, mullion windows and a large porch, with cartouche and sundial. In about 1800, it was converted into a hunting box for Sir Francis Burdett, the 3rd son of Sir Robert Burdett and his wife, Miss Sophia Coutts, of the famous banking family. It was almost ruinous, and Sir Robert more or less camped there.

From Derbyshire, Burdett was educated at Oxford and, whilst on a European tour, witnessed the early days of the French Revolution in Paris. Whilst most of the upper class lived in fear that England would suffer the same fate, this experience influenced the rest of Burdett's career. Soon after his marriage, he became an MP, known for his fiery oration and campaigns for reform. The man in the street saw him as a champion of free speech and a supporter of genuine grievances.

Sir Francis' first hunting appearance was at Great Dalby. He fell into a deep ditch and was rescued by George Brewitt. Contemporary writers describe Alfred Brocklehurst following over the ditch and, assuming Brewitt was a tenant farmer of Burdett's, shouted: "you damn fool Brewitt, why don't you sit on his head till he lowers your rent". This remark was typical of the landowners who never shared Burdett's concerns for the underprivileged.

His reformist speeches upset his fellow MPs and were a source of abuse in pamphlets of the time. He campaigned for parliamentary reform, *'since the sale of seats was openly avowed'*. *Cobbett's Register,* later *Hansard,* reported his speeches. On one occasion, Burdett's London home was forcibly entered and he was incarcerated in the Tower of London under close guard. Released through a side door, he missed the hero's welcome from his supporters outside.

Sir Francis published a letter warning of general unrest in the country and was charged with subversion. At Leicester Assizes, he was sentenced to 3 months in prison and fined £2,000. In 1819, Burdett's warnings materialised when 11 people were killed and over 400 wounded by the cavalry in arresting 'Orator' Hunt at Petersfield. An oak tree, replanted after a lightening strike, in Kirby Park is said to be where Burdett wrote his warning.

His youngest daughter, Angela Georgina Burdett-Coutts was the richest heiress in Europe and devoted herself to a life of philanthropy. She became known as the queen of the poor, giving away over £3 million during her lifetime. Queen Victoria made her a Baroness in 1871 and she became the first woman to be given the Freedom of the City of London.

In 1881, at the age of 67, she married her secretary who was forty years her junior.

Sir Francis was the exception to the rule amongst the hunting gentry. Credited with making free speech possible, he was given the nickname 'Old Glory'. He died from grief in 1844, ten days after his wife had passed away, having refused all food offered to him.

Cottage

Publications

This title is one in a new series by **Cottage Publications**.
For more information and to see our other titles, please visit our website
www.cottage-publications.com
or alternatively you can contact us as follows:–

Telephone: +44 (0)28 9188 8033
Fax: +44 (0)28 9188 8063

Cottage Publications
is an imprint of
Laurel Cottage Ltd.,
15 Ballyhay Road,
Donaghadee, Co. Down,
N. Ireland, BT21 0NG